CLAXTON

Also by Mark Cocker

LONELINESS AND TIME:
BRITISH TRAVEL WRITING IN THE TWENTIETH CENTURY

RIVERS OF BLOOD, RIVERS OF GOLD: EUROPE'S CONFLICT WITH TRIBAL PEOPLES

BIRDERS: TALES OF A TRIBE

BIRDS BRITANNICA

A TIGER IN THE SAND: SELECTED WRITINGS ON NATURE

CROW COUNTRY

BIRDS & PEOPLE (with David Tipling)

CLAXTON

Field Notes from a Small Planet

Mark Cocker

Illustrated by Jonathan Gibbs

JONATHAN CAPE
LONDON

Published by Jonathan Cape 2014

2 4 6 8 10 9 7 5 3 1

First published in Great Britain in 2014 by
Jonathan Cape
Random House, 20 Vauxhall Bridge Road,
London SW1V 2SA

www.vintage-books.co.uk

Addresses for companies within The Random House Group Limited can be found at:
www.randomhouse.co.uk/offices.htm

The Random House Group Limited Reg. No. 954009

A CIP catalogue record for this book is available from the British Library

ISBN 9780224099653

The Random House Group Limited supports the Forest Stewardship Council® (FSC®), the leading international forest-certification organisation. Our books carrying the FSC label are printed on FSC®-certified paper. FSC is the only forest-certification scheme supported by the leading environmental organisations, including Greenpeace. Our paper procurement policy can be found at www.randomhouse.co.uk/environment

FSC
www.fsc.org
MIX
Paper from responsible sources
FSC® C016897

Typeset in Centaur MT by Palimpsest Book Production Limited,
Falkirk, Stirlingshire

Printed and bound in Germany by GGP Media, GmbH Pößneck

For Dan and Gill

There can be no really black melancholy to him who lives in the midst of nature and has still his senses.

14 July 1845

It is a certain faeryland where we live. I wonder that I ever get five miles on my way, the walk is so crowded with events and phenomena. How many questions there are which I have not put to the inhabitants!

7 June 1851

The man of most science is the man most alive, whose life is the greatest event.

6 May 1854

Henry Thoreau, *The Journal*

CONTENTS

ACKNOWLEDGEMENTS

I am deeply grateful to the following editors for giving me an opportunity to write about my encounters with nature. They include the late Patrick Ensor (*Guardian Weekly*), Dominic Mitchell (*Birdwatch*), Steve Snelling (*Eastern Daily Press*), Celia Locks, Elisabeth Ribbans and Anne-Marie Conway (the *Guardian*) and Andrew McNeillie (*Archipelago*). I also give thanks to each of these publications for permission to reproduce my articles in book format. I am further indebted to Jonathan Gibbs for the deep care he has shown in producing the wonderful woodcut prints that accompany the text.

A number of people have helped me compile my list of species for *Claxton* over the last decade. They include Nigel Brown, Jon Clifton, Martin Collier, Ian Dawson, Chris and Ben Goldsmith, Tony Leech, Andy Musgrove, Jeremy Mynott, John O'Sullivan, Nick Owens, David Richmond, Tim Strudwick, Mark Telfer, Jim Wheeler and Ray Woods.

As always, this book involves the essential double act of my entire writing career, my agent Gill Coleridge and my editor Dan Franklin. I give them renewed thanks for their support and encouragement. I also owe deep thanks to the team at Random House – Clare Bullock, Neil Bradford and Joe Pickering – for all their hard work on the book. Finally, I wish to express immense gratitude to my 'girls' – my wife Mary Muir and our daughters Rachael and Miriam – for tolerating a household in which the sudden dash for binoculars, the alarm clock at dawn, or the presence of plant parts and bottles containing live moths and other sundry insects are all accepted as if they were routine elements in every normal family life.

INTRODUCTION

This book draws on writings produced over the last twelve years' residence in the small village of Claxton just a short distance to the east of Norwich. The 140 pieces were originally published in some form in newspapers, magazines or other books and anthologies (primarily the *Guardian*, *Guardian Weekly*, *Eastern Daily Press* and *Birdwatch* magazine). Yet I see them as very much more than a collection of journalism, and of all my books this has taken the longest to write.

The pieces are arranged in chronological order in twelve chapters, each of which covers a single month. They have been placed in sequence with priority given to the day (rather than the year) on which they were intended for publication so that in total they unfold as a diary portrait of Claxton through a single twelve-month period. I have also felt at liberty to change or add to the original versions, in some cases radically, on the basis that newspaper or magazine editors use material in order to meet their own internal requirements. Those needs are not necessarily in the best interests of the submitted text. I believe that an author has a right to revise or to improve earlier drafts in order to convey as truly as possible what was first intended.

Claxton is above everything a book about place, but it is also a celebration of the way in which a particular location can give shape and meaning to one's whole outlook. I view our original move from Norwich to Claxton as pivotal in my career. It happened in August 2001 and arose for professional reasons. At the time I had two columns on nature and wildlife in the *Guardian* and in the subscribers' sister title *Guardian Weekly*. Anybody who has ever written a regular article – a weekly or, heaven forbid, a daily piece – will tell you of the tyranny exercised by this particular master. There is no forgiveness for late copy, no reprieve for failure to deliver, no chance to suggest that nothing really moved you that week. The allocated print space has to be filled every time, and as soon as this is achieved the next deadline grinds towards you with inexorable, relentless speed.

In these circumstances most writers are playing what pundits call a percentage game: the best that they can do for as much of the time as possible. Not all pieces are perfect or even hit the correct note. From the 450 articles I've written for four such columns over the period since moving to Claxton I have selected less than a third. Of these, 85 per cent have been about wildlife seen in this parish. I have included material written about other locations, but I see these particular articles and the responses that they articulate as drawing inspiration in exactly the same way from residence in Claxton.

Before we moved here things were very different. In order to find subjects on which to write I had to drive my family every weekend, often both Saturdays and Sundays, rain or shine, winter or summer, usually to a coastal location and always to some wilder part of East Anglia. It involved much effort and it was perhaps a strain upon our children, although they seldom if ever complained. Being in the countryside was part of our family routine. It had the incidental benefits of allowing the children when they were very young to acquire vast pebble collections, or to renew their intimacies with favourite trees (in Holkham Park), or to revisit treasured swimming spots (Burnham Overy), to nose out premier blackberrying locations (Waxham) and – best of all – to enjoy the rewards of ice cream and cake at favourite cafés. All of this familial history flowed because in my peculiar line of work the countryside was my office.

By moving to Claxton I acquired an office of my own. Life changed overnight. Wildlife encounters entailed simply walking out of the front door and heading down Mill Lane across the marsh towards the river. I repeat that ritual now on a weekly and usually a daily basis. And almost always towards the river, to the Yare – like a divining rod, my instincts seem to propel me to the water. Sometimes, however, merely to go out into the garden is enough.

It is odd in a way that such a dry county as Norfolk is so defined by water. Yet it is a region most famous for its coast, lakes, rivers and marsh. It's often that strange paradox: a landscape best seen from a boat. At times Norfolk seems to be just water and sky; elemental layers in which terra firma hardly has a role. In the Yare Valley the ground beneath your feet has its origins in water.

My hope with this book is that readers might be inspired to look more closely at their own immediate surroundings, for, in many ways, there is little that is truly special about Claxton. Like most of the villages in this area, it comprises ordinary farmland. However, we divide its ground into what we call the 'uplands' and the marsh. The first word might conjure hilly places filled with contours, gradients and summits with high winds and views extending to the horizon. There are indeed vast panoramas to be had in Claxton, but they are from places on the twenty-metre contour line. These are our idea of 'uplands'. Really it is any ground above sea level. The land that lies at zero elevation, or thereabouts, is the part we know as the marsh.

It's not just at sea level, once it was sea: the final stretch of an inland arm of the *Oceanus Germanicus* that successive generations from the Romans onwards have wrestled out of the clutches of saltwater and into the estate of human agriculture. Claxton was once water and even now as dry land it retains many of the characteristics of water. It is level and it is large and it dwells under, and sometimes it feels oppressed by, vast skies. It's a landscape built in layers and in level planes of colour. At the uppermost tier is the feather-topped canopy of poplar or crack willow. A little lower is the fuller, richer, deep green of the distant woods: green mixed with white wherever sallow grows, but dark, almost bitter emerald if the dominant species is alder. Closer to the ground is the dense warm tan belt of old reed and lowest of all is the dead brown of old rush or the deep green of the new.

As well as level landscapes, I have a passion for routine. In Nepal in my early twenties I once ate the same meal every day for four months almost without variation: rice, dahl and spiced vegetables. I have a tendency towards music that unfolds very slowly: the compositions of Gavin Bryars (e.g. 'The Sinking of the Titanic') or The Necks (e.g. 'Sex'). The latter, an Australian jazz trio (about whom it was famously written that in their live performances anything can happen and seldom does), create songs that build steadily, patiently, minutely in rhythmic layers – like an incantation repeated inexorably until it triumphs over the listener – for more than an hour.

In order to know it properly a landscape requires routine and repetition. *Claxton* is a celebration of a relationship with place that has been built at a slow tempo. If ever one examines the processes of nature then very few of them happen in a hurry. A crocus or a daffodil freshly emerging from the ground in February never comes up faster than it should, despite one's wishing sometimes that it would. As it spreads across a field when at last the sun emerges from the clouds, that returning flood of sunlight will arrive at the spot where you stand steadily and entirely without haste. Nature keeps its own pace.

To do things routinely, to take the same walk time after time, is not to see the same view over and over. It is to notice the incremental rate of natural change and to appreciate that nothing is ever repeated. I am often struck by the way, when one has had some deeply memorable encounter with an otter, say, or perhaps a sighting of a rare bird or butterfly, that the next day you see almost nothing at all. They are never in the same spot. Nature has a way of balancing its books but it also has a way of avoiding duplicates. Every time it is unique. In this book I have included several pieces that cover the same basic theme, such as St Mark's flies, otters, swifts or peregrines. This is not just because each of the experiences filled me with a sense of something that had to be communicated; it's also because each one felt like the first time.

JANUARY

6 January 2013

Claxton

Because we have so drained the English landscape of any danger to ourselves, I think we easily overlook how potent a factor fear is in the lives of animals. In our parish, where peregrines and harriers are constantly back and forth on patrol, the flocks of lapwings and golden plovers often seem to spend their entire days merely standing and are almost without activity. Yet come darkness and the moon's rise the birds zigzag across the fields on those broad, strangely creaking wings to feed in its protective pale glow. You realise that daylight is all about vigilance and security, while night is the time to feed.

The natural accompaniment to all their days spent standing and watching are the plovers' weird convulsive dreads when, almost like an electric current, fear flushes over the whole flock and launches it skywards. Often one cannot find any genuine cause for these hair-trigger responses. Yet the simultaneity of it is astonishing, as is the beautifully coordinated sweep and flow of their movement. The dreads' impact upon our human senses and imagination is presumably similar to its effect on any predator. The viewer is at once mesmerised but confused by the manner in which so many different animals pool and sway as one. In fact, it so perplexed early ecologists that some even wondered if the birds were not capable of thought transference.

What we overlook perhaps is the rehearsals. Over thousands, and probably millions, of years, natural selection has favoured those birds with an ability to bury their identities and match precisely their movements to the actions of neighbours. Each generation slowly, cumulatively passed on the advantageous genes, but we forget the ragged processes and see only the flock's fine-honed finished machinery. It is strange to think that as we observe the amoeba-like globe of lapwings wheel and swerve in fantastic unity, we are connected to the instantaneous rush of their nerves and to the ancient time from which such wild perfection has been sculpted.

10 January 2011

CLAXTON

I open the door and straightaway can see the four metal rooks in our weathervane all tilting southwards. It may be a south wind but it is hard and sharp. It drives across the River Yare, and the great white steam billow rising above the sugarbeet factory at Cantley sails hard north-north-west for about a hundred metres, then drowns in that vast cold blast. The wind seems to brush through the valley and I am intrigued to note how even the swans, normally so immune to heat and cold, are all in the lee of an earth bank just south of a flight pond. At a distance they look like a last drift of snow heaped up against the black peat.

In the aftermath of last month's freeze the whole landscape has been burnt down to three basic colours. There is the leached green of the marsh itself and then the sedge brown to all the dyke edges and the patches of reed. Then finally there are the woodlands on every horizon. Superficially as I spin around they all seem black, but if I look harder there is a slightly warmer note mingled in, a faint purplish tone that is added in our area only by the alder trees. And there is no mistake: in aggregate the woods are actually puce coloured, precisely the same shade as an old scab.

For all this, as I walk by the Yare there is the faintest hint of change. Perhaps the reason for this lies entirely elsewhere:

our technical knowledge of the date and increment in the season. Perhaps it is the fact that the decorations are all now stowed and the pine needles swept away. Yet there is a sort of bright note in the air, hard to define or to lay to any cause, but it is there indisputably, and if I should give it a name, I wouldn't call it the start of spring. It is more the end of lifelessness.

11 January 2010

CLAXTON

The ice has steadily corralled the valley's flock of wigeon into ever-smaller areas of open water. At times two thousand birds are compressed into a dense mass along Claxton's main drain, and when they move into the fields they appear as a single dark slough of life in the hollows of the frozen marsh. On the one hand one senses how the stress of prolonged cold has left the birds more tolerant than usual of a close approach. On the other, and seemingly without good cause, the ducks are also extremely jittery. They bluster in broken wheeling showers from one part of the river to the next. Then, just as inexplicably, they will rise off the Yare altogether and flop into the adjacent dykes. Nothing seems to settle the collective mood.

I love the way they take flight in a prolonged even sequence, so that they peel off the water as a continuous blanket that instantly atomises and falls back to earth amid a downpour of contact notes. The sound of wigeon is a soft high whistling rather like the breathy note one instinctively makes when told of some startling revelation. Multiply the sound by a thousand and it becomes a tide of music filled with a sense of mildness, innocence and confusion. Yet it also carries other potential resonances. The sound beautifully evokes both place and weather. It seems indivisible from wind and open landscapes where the horizon is distant and the space immense. One cannot imagine a wigeon has ever heard its voice bounce off some solid topography as an echo, except perhaps during that luxurious fortnight cocooned in the egg beneath its mother's breast. By the same token, one cannot conceive how the adult wigeon can ever produce its questioning note and not be instantly reassured by a neighbour's reply. So wigeon song is at once a song of open space but also of companionability. It is also the defining soundtrack for this parish in winter.

12 January 2009

CLAXTON

It was one of those glorious anticyclonic winter days when you sense that there is not a mote of dust in the entire troposphere. Not only could you see with enhanced clarity in the crystalline air, but your sense of hearing seemed to acquire a higher level of acuity. I picked out the calls of Bewick's swans long before I saw them. They came from the south-east, out of the direct sunlight. Yet even as sharply cut, sun-burnt silhouettes, they never looked completely black, but appeared a muted grey. There were twenty-four birds in a single line vocalising constantly as they approached.

The sound of wild swans is one of the glories of the European winter. The Bewick's call is an unhurried, soft, almost woodwind, pigeon-like sound that has a relaxed, random quality rather resembling wind chimes. The sound of one bird 'bumps' into the responses of its neighbours and these near-sequential notes unfold across the open space of Claxton Marsh as a gentle aerial winter song.

At one point they looked as if they were going to land and several birds drew in slightly and deepened the downward arch of their unflapping wings, so that they stalled in speed yet retained height. The pause allowed them to assess conditions below, where something – alas – made them decide not to land awhile in our fields. Instead they described a slow figure of eight across the sky and banked to head upriver. This freshly chosen objective introduced a slight urgency into the flight calls, which now sounded wilder, more yelping, almost suggesting the clanging notes of cranes or perhaps the baying of distant hounds.

Bewick's swans are not rare in the Yare Valley. I see small numbers in most years, but there are nothing like the flocks that occur further north in the main Broads area, nor the huge congregations that gather on the Norfolk–Cambridgeshire border. Every sighting here is an occasion and I savoured their woodwind music until it faded eventually back into the customary Claxton silence.

14 January 2008

SURLINGHAM, NORFOLK

The huge oak tree lying on its side is soft and spongy to the touch and with my thumbnail I can drive right into the heartwood. In fact, it seems as much a labyrinth of beetle-gnawed cavities as it is solid fibre. Yet for once the natural insignia connoting decay and the passage of time are overshadowed by the human structure that stands nearby. St Saviour's Church was probably already a ruin when this oak was a young tree. The building's own roots go back to the early Norman period and archaeological work suggests that its construction may have been contemporaneous with the building of Norwich Cathedral. However, in the late Middle Ages, the village of Surlingham climbed over the hill and then vanished down the other side, leaving St Saviour's alone and neglected. Eventually the round-towered St Mary's eclipsed its neighbour as the place of worship and St Saviour's was left to settle into a prolonged decline.

In the early modern period its tower collapsed. In the nineteenth century the roof vanished, and where the pews once stood rises a tangle of nettle, bramble and other faithful attendants of human indifference. Long sections of the flint wall have also gone and only the chancel arch, soaring now upwards to a roofless space, gives any hint of human aspiration at the site.

Wild rabbits, which would have been almost unknown in Britain when St Saviour's was first built, have riddled the remains of the chancel wall with deep holes. In my imagination I follow the animals down their burrows and where they now scratch their fleas are the earliest stones ever laid at the church. I think of the medieval labourers who placed them there and I wonder what they might have done had I told them what is now established fact: that the black flint lumps in their hands, carefully slotted into the walls layer by layer, were once sea urchins and sponges living in the warm tropical waters that stood over this spot about eighty million years ago.

16 January 2006

CLAXTON

Although it was not yet light I could tell that dawn was coming by the way that the headlights no longer carved their clean-edged tunnel through the darkness. And by the time I approached the river, the outlines of the bare trees were disentangling themselves from night, emerging as a greyish aura of branches around the main trunk. The only sound, bar the rush of the cold rain-laden southerlies, was a mallard quacking on the water. It sailed with the current on the sweeping meander that appeared in the half light as a grey twisting sheet of tin.

I looked north across the valley and on into the southern 'uplands' of the Broads, where Buckenham Carrs formed a dark mass on the horizon. With each passing minute the marsh landscape brightened by degrees, and while wigeon were now whistling loudly, the first real sign of daytime was a small group of black-headed gulls, their whiteness razoring an arrow formation as they angled upstream. Then the lapwings started to arrive, the tight flocks showing as thick dark lines across the sky. But the unexpected highlight of my dawn vigil was the pink-footed geese that flew towards me in several loose skeins.

The population of this goose species, which breeds predominantly in Iceland, has increased constantly in the past few years, and there are now 150,000, half the world's total, wintering in Norfolk. The occurrence of pinkfeet in the Yare Valley, including this small flock before me, is a measure of their range expansion. The skeins coalesced about midfield, and, while it may seem strange to suggest it, the first light of morning caught the pale leading edges of their wings as they came down almost vertically; and against the wider blur of their beating – one fine silvery line seeming to link to the next – they reminded me just momentarily of a spider's web frosted with dew.

18 January 2010

Claxton

Twice recently I've been asked to nominate what I consider to be the best books on nature and birds, and twice I've felt I had to pass. I believe strongly that books are reactive agents, to which our responses change over time or in relation to other books, and I don't like to try to rank what seem themselves living ecological entities. It would be like trying to choose, for instance, blackbird before ring ouzel.

But if I were forced to make a selection at gunpoint then I would have no hesitation in naming the works of J. A. Baker (1926–1987). His two books *The Peregrine* (1967) and *The Hill of Summer* (1969), published to great acclaim, are less well known today. Fortunately, Baker has undergone a recent revival with writers of all kinds, including Poet Laureate Andrew Motion and television presenter Simon King, acknowledging Baker's influence upon them. A paperback of his first book was reissued in 2005 and this year his original publishers HarperCollins are producing a hardback containing both Baker's published works and his hitherto unpublished diaries.

Baker the man was a rather elusive figure. He started birding in the late fifties and was especially active in the 1960s, cleaving strongly to a small bicycle-covered radius of sites around Chelmsford in Essex. Danbury Hill and the marshes of the Blackwater Estuary were two favourite haunts. Even in his close focus on a small territory, Baker seems to be highly relevant to our own carbon-sensitive age, providing a model of how one can find inspiration and satisfaction in a very local avifauna.

What rings clearest in his writings is Baker's decade-long fixation with one bird, the peregrine. We have to recall what seems now a very ancient past when late-twentieth-century environmentalists even feared for the global survival of this supremely dramatic predator. Baker, believing presumably that he was witness to the final act in the peregrine's great tragedy on earth, relentlessly tracked the birds wintering in his Essex patch.

A loner by nature, Baker seems not to have forged strong links with other Essex birders and his string of records concerning peregrines in the sixties aroused his peers' suspicions. Even today, Simon Wood, author of the excellent, meticulous *The Birds of Essex*, has had sufficient qualms over Baker's peregrine records to note how the editors of the 1968 Essex bird report wondered whether he was seeing birds of non-wild origin.

The problem possibly lies in the difference between the literal truth of birders' notebooks and the literary truth as expressed by Baker. In both his works the author stripped out place names, exact dates (he gives the day and month but not the year), any reference to people, even to himself, so that it is very difficult to fix precisely the where, when, how or why of Baker's descriptions. What one is left with, however, is a sort of mythic story of quest for an almost mythic bird that has universal resonances.

The strangest and most ironic thing of all about the whiff of fraud hanging over Baker's Essex masterpiece is that the whole book is shot through with an authenticity of tone, a truthfulness to the experience of birds and landscape, that has few rivals not just in Britain but in the English-speaking world. Anybody who has ever attempted to go beyond a mere list of birds and express something of what they feel about their encounters with wild creatures in places they know and love would profit from a literary visit to Baker's Essex. As far as I am able to judge, nobody has found a simpler, truer, more original, more precise language for these experiences than this former employee of the Automobile Association.

Here is just a sample of Baker's words. In *The Hill of Summer* he describes a churring nightjar 'breathing out the dark snake of his song to fork and flicker at the moon'. He hears the 'daffodil richness of a blackbird's pondering voice'; and, elsewhere, 'Many blackbirds sang, a rambling music, like sunlit summer rain.' How about this for trees in a gale: 'The whole wood is an exultant respiration of storm-driven wind and rain. It is like being inside the hollow bones of an immense bird, listening to the sudden inrush of the air and the measured heart-beat of huge wings.' And finally, here's Baker on the weirdness of thick-knees: 'One by one the calls of stone curlews rose in the long valleys of the downs, like fossil voices released from the strata of the chalk . . . shaping upon the darkness a stonehenge of haunting sound.'

Baker was more than a poet. He was a naturalist with supreme powers of observation and linguistic exactitude. I wouldn't want to suggest, however, that he is an easy read. He is not. The writing can be dense or slow-going. Like medicine, it needs to be consumed in small doses. But taken in the correct measure there are few tonics with the power to renew our zest for birds and nature than the glorious words of John Alec Baker.

21 January 2006

HOLKHAM, NORFOLK

'This is really the best place to see lions. Where you can see them how they're meant to be. Where they're in their true state. Here the lions are really wild.' I remember the words clearly.

They were English words but pronounced in that exotic, awkward, chiselled tone of the Afrikaans speaker. He was a South African professional big game hunter, working in a part of a Botswanan national park that was licensed for sportsmen to come to shoot wild animals, including a small number of lions. The licence fees were extremely high and the hunting strictly regulated, so that the revenue derived from the death of a few lions, however distasteful that may seem to many of us, helped finance the wider conservation of Botswana's wonderful wildlife. To me it seemed a reasonable arrangement, especially in a country as relatively poor as Botswana.

But the part of the professional hunter's case that I queried then, and challenge now, was the notion that only in his sector of the park were the lions really wild. I think we know what he meant. In the protected areas where they are not hunted the lion prides become habituated to a constant wagon train of land cruisers, and eventually they behave as if the intruding humans never existed, no matter how closely they approach. Yet in the shooting concession areas the lions run away at the merest glimpse of humans. However, my point would be that the lions aren't wild. In shrinking from contact with humans, the big cats are not expressing some innately hostile spirit that is fundamental to their nature. They are simply frightened – frightened for their lives. Fear and wildness, however, are not the same things.

I'm reminded of that conversation every time I visit north Norfolk in winter, because in a way the same scenario is played out on the grazing marshes around the coast. Head down the track known as Lady Ann's Drive at Holkham beach and you cannot fail to notice the huge flocks of wild geese that are spread across the fields on both sides. Or perhaps I should rephrase that, because the geese look so contented, so nonchalant about the human traffic, that a visitor could easily overlook them, assuming that they were merely wildfowl in an ornamental collection. But the pink-footed geese that are so abundant on that part of the coast are as wild as they get.

They come to us in late autumn from their breeding grounds on the east coast of Greenland, but especially from the dark lava fields of central Iceland, where they nest in sometimes dense colonies close to the mountain ice caps. Frequently they like to build their circular nest mounds of breast down and vegetation, which build up year on year, by the edge of a cliff, where the gander keeps tight watch on his brooding partner to protect her from Arctic foxes.

So when the great dark skeins of geese arrive in Norfolk I find the clamour of their beautiful, resonant, dog-like calls filled with a sense of northern wilderness. They are, it is true, without fear of the humans with whom they share the Norfolk coast because they are no longer hunted in protected areas like Holkham National Nature Reserve. But I like to think that it is not the geese that have lost their wildness, it is we who have acquired it; or, rather, we have acquired a passionate commitment to their wildness. It appeals to and fulfils something within us. The geese are, in a sense, a symbol of a reawakened reverence for life beyond our own species and outside our prescription.

The human-tolerant goose flocks of north Norfolk – no less than the sleepy and complacent lions of the Okavango national parks – express at least one success of our conservation policies. There are now 150,000 pink-footed geese wintering in Norfolk and every season those dark skeins across the sky spread their calls ever wider, partly helped by fields full of sugar beet, whose green unharvested tops have become a major part of their diet. Some of the single roost flocks coming for the night to Scolt Head Island have numbered eighty thousand. Imagine it: two hundred tonnes of feather and sinew all descending in one great rush of wings and hammering hearts. The county has become the setting for one of the great wildlife spectacles in Britain. Norfolk as a whole is now the winter destination for about half the entire global population of pink-footed geese.

The other day I caught just a small fraction of this

magnificent concentration of birds as the geese came in to roost on the marshes to the west of Lady Ann's Drive. Some were already landing in front of us and were joining the ever-expanding mass, which spread across the fields as a solid carpet of long-necked birds. But across the heavens through the entire 180-degree panorama we could see skein after skein, the nearer birds superimposed upon the more distant flocks so that the bare sky was crazed with the sequence of their lines. Order was shattered and that ever-changing vision of wing-quickened chaos was matched by a glorious recessional of their calls that faded back into the sour north wind.

Those birds of the far north have the power to transform the atmosphere of the entire landscape. They made north Norfolk, that fundamentally humanised place, a more interesting and fulfilling country. They brought some other rare element to it and aroused a richer sense of what life can be. Perhaps it is the meeting of these two elements – the outer and the inner life – that we should really call 'the wild'.

23 January 2012

CLAXTON

Under the big oaks by the gate to the marsh the drizzle feels less, but the gloom is worse. The whole sky is deep pencil-lead grey, except for a slit of brighter cloud on the northern horizon. The light and the rain mean that I see the dozen or so reed buntings flitting along the dyke even more poorly than usual. They always move as I pass in staggered sequence, the nearest triggering a neighbour's flight, so that they register not as one flock, but as an aggregate of half-seen individuals. Even this understates the fragmentary nature of my daily encounters with the birds. In truth I have barely seen one whole reed bunting all winter. The lattice of willow whips along the dyke breaks them down so that they are always revealed as an angular, cubist tangle of glimpses – a wing here, the flirting white bars of a tail there, and a head and shoulders poked cleanly from a perch as one stops momentarily to grill the intruder.

Occasionally in high spring a singing male reed bunting will stand out in full sunlight, the plum-like black head sharp within its blossom-white rosette. More typically, however, the species retains about itself an aura of self-effacement, as if it had a sense that it is too dull in colour and tuneless in voice to warrant full attention. Yet this much reed buntings proclaim loudly about our experience of nature. So many of our living neighbours – the leafless trees, the dank grasses and flowerless plants, the expiring fungi and voiceless birds – hardly ever acquire the foreground of our minds. Yet every single one of them is integral to that magical uplift in spirits, which is the great gift of a walk in wild space. Without the reed buntings we would not notice so keenly the crack in the sky and that widening pasture of blue. Nor would we feel so blessed by the warmth of that sun in our faces.

24 January 2011

CLAXTON

I normally find them rootling in the reeds along Carleton Beck and in this post-Christmas soft spell it makes me want to clench my fist and wave it at the heavens, as a salute to their winter survival. For the bearded tits were there all through that grinding deadness of last year's freeze.

Each day I'd see them at the same spot. One bird would suddenly let out a sharp ringing ping sound that always seemed to startle its owner as much as me. Then two birds, usually two, would shuffle up the reeds simultaneously and take me in with those fierce and faintly exotic lemon eyes, and carry on feeding. In that world of white they seemed even more beautiful: that soft dove-like blue-grey of his crown, and the rich warm ginger of their upperparts.

Even when they are buried in cover, one can follow bearded tits by that self-reassuring conversation of sharp notes. Otherwise they signal their whereabouts with mouse-like twitchings of the vegetation. Suddenly up will pop that amusing male's head with its extravagant black whiskers that look one part pantomime villain, one part Buddhist sage. The moustache is broadest around the eyes and tapers to long waxed tips either side of the throat. One detail you seldom learn from looking in the bird book is the way those whiskers actually stand proud of the facial plumage like a real moustache.

Bearded tits may carry with them a note of humour but there is nothing comic about their presence at today's sunlit lark-song-filled moment. I recall once watching these birds and in the adjacent dyke a swan, six hundred times heavier, lumbered through the ice-smeared water, progressing one painful lunge at a time so that the glass-like sheet splintered with each new effort. It was four in the afternoon. There were sixteen hours of darkness ahead. It was minus ten. Each night I asked the same thing: how on earth did any of them make it?

25 January 2010

CLAXTON

The tiny gestures of spring are building incrementally in our parish. The first was the wheezing two-note song of a great tit, like a see-saw pivoting on its unoiled fulcrum. Then dunnock added a thin pleasing tinkle to the grey dawn, and this week I heard the unmistakable drumming of a great spotted woodpecker. How can anything so small and dry as this mechanical note be joyous? And yet the simple rap of a beak on dead wood, which is chosen specifically for its powers of amplification, hits the ear with enormous impact. The announcement of that emphatic 'yes' is the first moment we know absolutely that the whole panorama of life will open very soon.

A sound I love equally is a speciality of our area. Chinese water deer bark at night as a means of communication – an arc of shrill scream that bridges their otherwise solitary lives – but it also marks their season of rut. So the noise is a love note. One has largely to imagine the acts of tenderness and procreation because one seldom sees two deer in close contact during daylight hours. You normally spot them feeding right out in the middle of the marsh and safe from disturbance. Occasionally, however, you can catch them unawares. They seem extremely short-sighted and if you stand absolutely still they stare hard and quizzically, their teddy-bear ears batting back and forth to catch some scintilla of sound, their downward-pointing tusks adding a note of comic villainy to their otherwise sweet faces. Then they turn and bound away, full bottomed, bustling forward in shallow undulations as if they have to thread their bodies through small gaps in the thin air. They are not graceful. Yet there is a beautiful economy to this manner in which they drive a wedge between the breeze. With each leap and as the forelimbs touch down, that motion is followed instantaneously by a hinging upwards and forwards of their thick, powerful haunches.

26 January 2009

CLAXTON

I can see it now: a bird with a wingspan the length of a barn door swooping across the marshes and lifting a goose in its massive talons. The predator is a white-tailed eagle. My image of it, alas, is merely a vision. Yet the dream has moved a step closer to reality now that Natural England proposes to reintroduce the species to the Norfolk coast. It follows a number of English release projects involving ospreys and red kites. The efforts to boost numbers of the latter have been particularly successful and restored to us one of our most charismatic birds. The scheme involving the eagle, however, is a step up in terms of ambition.

The restoration of the white-tailed eagle in such a densely crowded part of Britain challenges our national tendency towards anxiety about wildness in nature. Yet, if successful, it would underscore our preparedness to share the landscape with other creatures. Because to make room for white-tailed eagles would no doubt necessitate that we slacken a little our tight grip over the countryside. We would perhaps lose a little but we might gain immeasurably.

There is opposition to the scheme even among naturalists, which is fascinating for what it says about ourselves. The arguments cluster around a perception of eagles as being synonymous with wild, remote, northern uplands. Opponents scan the ornithological texts and can find little proof of its former residence here. Yet place-name evidence and archaeological data indicate that eagles were once widespread across southern England. On the Continent, high densities of the birds occur in low-lying wetland environments very similar to East Anglia. Its present British confinement to remotest Scotland is evidence not of the bird's love for mountain scenery, but of centuries of human persecution. The restoration of eagles requires that we re-imagine the bird less as an icon of wilderness and more as our near neighbour. In so doing we will recover something wild and precious in the landscape and also something important within ourselves.

29 January 2007

NKOB, MOROCCO

It is twenty-eight years since I last visited this place, which is famous as the town with more kasbahs (fortified houses) than any other in the country. I was frustrated to find that neither the desert scenery nor the dark Anti-Atlas mountains looming way to the north roused more than a flicker of recognition. Occasionally I'd get a fleeting sense of congruence between the present landscape and some memory lost deep within me, but I never achieved any cinematic-style rerun of the past that allowed me to appreciate here was the spot where we had done this, there was the place we had seen that.

Yet how could I forget it? From across the stony wadi, the town's outline presented a wonderful vision. A dense tessellation of camel-toned mud walls was pressed together above the brilliant greenery of Nkob's palmery. It always strikes me as remarkable how long human residence in a place allows the occupants to distil not only the most practical structures but also buildings that seem uniquely blended to their wider aesthetic context. Nkob is a classic example. Even the vegetable gardens – a complex of early crops, dividing mud walls and gushing channels of fresh water, roofed by swaying palm leaves – seemed designed with beauty in mind.

Fortunately I do have one photograph from my original visit, a print depicting two young boys taking it in turns to stand in a well and douse the other with buckets of cold water. It instantly brings back the breathless 40-degree-centigrade heat of that August afternoon, but it also dislodges one further Nkob memory: the sight of a snake, probably a cobra, zigzagging through the palm groves and the sound of birds – bulbuls and babblers – all around. On the recent cloudy morning, however, the air was deliciously cool while the only movement was the chiffchaffs sallying for gnats amid the greenery. It was deeply moving to think that in six weeks' time those same birds will be singing from the treetops in Claxton.

FEBRUARY

February 2009

The most recent review book to arrive with a loud thump on the doormat is a large, beautiful tome entitled *Great Birds of Britain and Europe* by Jonathan Elphick and David Tipling. As one might expect from two top creators of the birding world, the book is a blend of high-quality writing and photographs that focuses on the continent's two hundred most charismatic species.

As Elphick and Tipling freely acknowledge, the central question underlying a book of this kind is how does one define what are the region's star species. In the end, won't each of us have a profoundly individual take on what constitutes a 'great' bird? The book is wonderfully engaging, partly because it asks questions about the way that we all subconsciously make judgements about our wildlife experiences. Why do we value our encounters with barn owls more than those with blue tits?

A key criterion one can see at work in the selection, which is the authors' attempt to second-guess our own choices, is the issue of abundance. Generally, birds that are scarce or less frequently encountered are assumed to galvanise our imaginations more than their commoner siblings. For example, black vulture and ring ouzel are among the golden two hundred, while griffon vulture and common blackbird are not. Barn swallow and house martin didn't quite make the cut, but red-rumped swallow and crag martin did.

Using abundance as a measure of charisma is understandable. A preoccupation with the exceptional is almost hardwired into the human imagination. We always, it seems, prefer the Fabergé egg or the Maserati before the Christmas-cracker trinket or the Skoda estate. In birdwatching rarity has its own particular allure. Whenever we encounter something scarce or just inherently difficult to observe we tend to look harder. Think, for instance, of the generic fascination exercised by owls (which have a whopping representation in the book of nine species!). By looking harder and longer the experience becomes imprinted on our memories. It seems to be a more fulfilling encounter, precisely because we bring to that moment a deeper quality of attention and, if you like, more of ourselves.

Pondering this issue as one soaks up the fine words and images is part of the fun of the book. However, locked away inside the question of why we choose the scarce before the commonplace is a more important social and political concern. In the sphere of conservation I sense that our inherent orientation towards the rare has often distorted the way in which we look at the environment.

How often one finds conservation policies built around a few charismatic species, such as the tiger, polar bear or, more parochially, the Eurasian bittern or corncrake. Singling out the flagship animal is often a way of simplifying a project for public consumption, making complex ecologies easier to understand for the layperson. Yet the downside is it continues to reinforce the idea of the charismatic few. When what truly makes an ecosystem flourish is the very opposite of its flagship representative: the sheer bio-luxuriance of its commonest constituents – usually the plants and myriad invertebrates. A reedbed doesn't amount to very much without its multiple millions of phragmites' stems.

The nature reserve is in many ways an analogue of the rare creature. It is a special place where the important wildlife is cordoned off from – and there's that word again – the 'commonplace' environment. Unfortunately the nature reserve not only protects the rare creature, it has also preserved intact the overloaded value that we have attached to rarity since the very origins of conservation. The drive to secure a meaningful environment in this country began partly with the efforts of a few pioneers to protect the large copper butterfly in East Anglia from imminent extinction. We have never really deviated from that basic model ever since.

If, however, we had set out to preserve what is most distinctive but commonplace in each location, then we may have secured a more viable version of the British landscape. If we had set aside in every parish, in every county, a tithe for nature – a viable portion of the land where what was common was maintained in a state of bio-luxuriance – then we might well have avoided the present state of affairs, where the house sparrow, common starling, lapwing and grey partridge are among our most threatened birds.

It is not too late to restate the importance of the commonplace in environmental protection. There is still scope to implement a bottom-upwards version of the countryside. But it requires us to select a very different kind of flagship species. I have a few suggestions for starters. How about the oak tree, the gorse bush, the bumblebee, common frog and common blackbird?

4 February 2013

CLAXTON

Every sighting of an owl is a gift. I feel I must stop to enjoy it as a way of giving thanks. But what if, as happened here for the entire fortnight of snow, there are owls every few paces. The total on the marsh was twelve, but my maximum during any lunchtime walk was ten. I was stopping every few minutes and even, sometimes, every few seconds to savour the next wonderful encounter. A walk of one kilometre was taking two hours. The lunchtime break was expanding to absorb half the afternoon. But then who would take such a gift for granted? Now the snow's gone, so have all the owls.

The most powerful part of the experience was the way the birds seemed to change to capture the elements of place more completely. The marsh was reduced to two tones – the white of the snow and the sedge brown of standing vegetation. These constituents mirrored precisely the colours in the birds and it was extraordinary to see how the short-eared owls' underwings acquired a beautiful silky sheen echoing the snow-covered fields to perfection. And if the short-eared owls' undersides turned white, then the barn owls' shone silver.

There is a level at which the owls are truly the landscape distilled. Beneath every square metre of ground are ten million million bacteria or actinomycetes, ten thousand million protozoa and five million nematodes. They in turn create the soil that supplies the grasses. The vegetation feeds the voles and the voles nourish the owls. So the birds are genuinely the land converted to soundless silk-winged animation. There was another way in which I caught these visitors as reflections of place. I was taking a photograph of snow-clad Carleton Beck and at precisely the moment the shutter closed a barn owl was mirrored by the water. I look at the image now and it is as if the landscape and the stream were caught by chance amid their own owl dreams.

6 February 2012

NORWICH

The sky was anti-freeze blue and there was white frost on all the molehills, but about fifty people had braved the midday cold. We were there officially to open a fabulous new nature trail, the work of a group at the University of East Anglia, which is one of those institutions that is thrice blessed in terms of its location. The River Yare passes a small lake just south of the campus and both are surrounded by a glorious marsh and wood. Few universities boast the kind of doorstep biodiversity that UEA enjoys and while most folk strolling the paths focus on the kingfishers and grebes on the open water, the whole site is home to 2,500 recorded species. Ecology lecturer Iain Barr puts the probable total at over 5,000 species but it certainly includes several hundred beetles, more than 400 fungi and 650 moth species.

By their very nature, interpretation boards on these sorts of trails depict only a tiny sample of the wildlife present. They usually focus on highly charismatic creatures and, as one might expect, the beautiful new signs at UEA concentrate on the grebes and that other stock attraction at wetland sites, the otter. I always feel otters are listed to keep us all looking. Everyone hopes to see one but precious few ever do. However, this was one of those occasions when nature upstaged not only the nature trail and the nature-trail board, but even the official opening of the nature trail. A young otter, one of last year's litter, chose the middle of my speech to launch herself out of the water and into the winter sunlight in front of the assembled crowd. I'm sure I wasn't the only one to suspect some devilish stunt. But no, there she was, unscripted and totally unexpected, amid a gush of oohs and aahs, porpoising freely like a swallow through the spring air. The speeches may have been a stop–start affair but the trail itself truly opened with a splash.

7 February 2011

BUCKENHAM CARRS, NORFOLK

The rooks and jackdaws that gather nightly to roost at this spot through the winter seem to be more numerous than ever this year and we were hoping for a good show. The birds first assemble on fields next to the wood in which they pass the night, although the exact spot for the pre-roost muster varies according to human disturbance or the birds' own simple whim. Tonight they were using two separate places.

As daylight ebbed away about ten thousand swirled down to an expanse of recently ploughed ground sloping towards us. The force-five south wind made them playful and more vocal than ever. The stream of new arrivals sent on ahead of itself a great surge tide of gravel and flint notes that sparked excitement among its fellows. Pitching down from on high, these fresh rooks and jackdaws seemed suddenly to release themselves from the plodding measured beat of normal corvid flight. And they fell earthwards, almost uncontrollably, so that they reminded me of some last bonfire of a lifetime's papers, each charred page rising, falling and twisting in the vent of boiled air.

Then at the witching hour when all birds had come they flew for the trees to sleep. Two flocks, maybe fifty thousand in all, converged. They rose up above the wood and pitched convulsively back and forth, the flock compressing and then instantly breaking apart once more. The lower contours of this mass were ragged and asymmetrical, but I noticed that the upper line of the whole flock possessed momentarily a sweet curve like the upturned hull of a ship. As one, the birds sank inexorably into the deeper cold black of the trees. A member of our group remarked that had they been placed here blindfold and made to name that immense upsurge of crow music, all their individual notes blended to one element, it would suggest nothing more closely than the Niagara roar of some vast waterfall.

8 February 2010

CLAXTON

A pair of peregrines, almost resident now in our neighbourhood, have made things lively for the last week. Twice I've watched the male hunting with real intent. It came down first among a flock of wigeon. The powerful regularity of a falcon's usual overhead patrolling flight was exchanged for movements of extraordinary purpose. The wings were in-drawn, the beat was intermittent and almost flickering. At such a long range, this newly acquired profile reminded me rather of a swallow's when hawking insects. Simultaneously the compression of the wings against the body made it seem as if it had just gained weight and gravity was now pulling it forward and down.

Wigeon themselves are no mean fliers. On the wing they look slender, curvy and stylish, with a particularly sweet ellipse from the mid-belly to the pointed tail that renders a relative like the mallard squat and coarse in comparison. Yet the peregrine's acceleration into the wigeon left them looking static. The way the flock shattered and the ducks flung themselves wildly either side of the peregrine's trajectory created a scene like a whip cracking across dusty ground, or a pile of iron filings suddenly pulled apart by magnets from opposing sides. Somehow the wigeon emerged unscathed.

The gap between the prowess of hunter and hunted was even more pronounced when the target was a wood pigeon. The same tiercel surged towards it, pouring forward with that liquid quality of a hunting shark. The way it overtook the pigeon made me feel sure I was about to see my first ever peregrine kill. Then down it came at the angle of a stabbing blade, not once but three times. The third time I was certain that there had been contact between the two and the pigeon fell away, while the peregrine swung up into mid-air. Yet it had failed again and it came down itself to earth in a long curving descent like a fish returning to the streambed.

13 February 2006

SOTTERLEY PARK, SUFFOLK

There were twelve blackbirds spread across a large sunken dell that was covered with dead foliage from a number of ancient oaks. The birds were so intent on foraging that some were virtually buried beneath the leaf litter and at a glance it looked like a uniformly copper-coloured bowl without any signs of life. Yet if I closed my eyes, their combined leaf-turning actions created the sound of some wonderfully light-footed being moving across the woodland floor.

Through the telescope there was no mistaking the blackbirds' shiny elderberry eyes, nor the gleaming black of the males' plumage. It was intriguing to see how all fed in the same manner: a couple of bounds forward accompanied by a vigorous sideways sweeping action with the crocus-coloured bill. The meticulous industry around their efforts made them seem like the park's self-appointed archivists, carefully unearthing then simultaneously reburying the secrets of the wood.

Blackbirds are so deeply embedded in our experience of the landscape that they are a kind of English history all by themselves. I cannot think of dramatic scenes from our past without the bird being caught, as it were, in the corner of the frame. I see them, for instance, glancing up from leaf-tossing exercises as Harold's dogged thanes march the Weald to their fate at Hastings. Or, as the German fighters and bombers went over in 1940, I can hear the engines' drone trigger that sharp hysterical blackbird note, which always seems to sound like metal shards accumulating flake by flake on a metal floor.

In a way both the men in the air and those on the ground were fighting for the blackbird, because just as much as the bird's soft mellifluous song is entwined with our sense of the soil, so it was, even unconsciously, for the Germans. For blackbirds are part of our great European heritage and behind the actions and sounds of each one is our shared past heaped up like bullion, or, perhaps, like so many dead leaves.

20 February 2012

CLAXTON

The ice-edged easterlies brought their own kind of harvest to our parish. I climbed up the Yare riverbank and there on the water were three goosander, the male a glorious mix of emerald and salmon-blushed white. Alas, my appearance spooked them and their feet clattered the surface as they rose, his breast reflected on it as a shimmering patch of icy white, and then they were gone.

I haven't seen goosander since the spring and that encounter couldn't have been more different. I'd stopped at Llyn Dinas just east of Beddgelert in Snowdonia, amid a downpour of soft warm spring rain. My poolside walk coincided with the moment that a female goosander and fourteen freshly hatched ducklings were heading for the safety of open water. At times she was carrying three of the brood upon her back, the smooth low-loaded contours of her own mantle lending itself to this kind of hitch-hiking. The young had an aura of exquisite innocence. Small orange flanges at the corners of their minuscule beaks gave them a down-turned sadness about the mouth, and occasionally one caught the intense vulnerability of their lemon belly down as they jinked and puttered upstream.

The female talked all the time to her brood with a soft 'grrrr' note that intensified when I got too close, but all anxieties were finally smoothed out as they attained the green-shaded sanctity of the pool. Instantly those 30-gram ducklings all fresh to the world began to sally after fish fry and were immediately lost in tiny bubbles of intense new experience. They threw themselves into it, diving just beneath the meniscus so that they ploughed ahead of themselves a grey-white pulse of surface water, while in their wake was a fizzing spray. In that very moment they knew exactly what they were and why they had hatched. They criss-crossed one another's paths in a kind of frenzied chaos but through all their movements one sensed the deep pure sense of self within them.

21 February 2011

CLAXTON

It may be a projection of my own sense of seasonal change – such as the crocuses in our hedge and the song thrush shouting from the wood – but I can't help thinking that there is a definite edginess in the birds gathered on the Yare floodplain. It is as if they know themselves that it's in the air – a kind of pre-migration tension – and it will soon well up and drive these wigeon and lapwings north for their breeding grounds.

The mood is stirred further by a male peregrine, who rises above the woods and glides south so slowly and smoothly that it feels as if I'm watching not a distant physical object but a floater passing gently down the curve of my own iris. The anxiety among all the five thousand ducks and waders across the marsh wells up in a great symphony of flight. Momentarily their lives are shaped by and answer to the beating of one falcon's heart and I wonder how we should process morally that all this glorious spectacle of the rising flocks is a product of raw fear? Can something so dreadful truly be so beautiful?

The most compelling part comes when about two thousand lapwings lift in a single elongated group that is convex in shape. As they rise so their upper wings are tilted towards me like a billowing sheet of black. Then, as one, they present their undersides and rise higher in a broken veil of white. From below and almost through the middle of these lapwings blasts a denser flock of wigeon with even greater urgency. They cross. I can hear all the woodwind chaos of their wings. Out of this terror they build upwards into a great momentary cathedral of birds and the peregrine, shining powder-blue even in this flat light, twists down upon them. Yet he fails. They scatter and in sub-groups slowly they simmer back down until all are once again spread across the marsh. Still nothing has happened.

22 February 2010

Monsal Dale, Derbyshire

Whenever I think of ash trees I think of their deep generosity. This is not just special pleading for the logs that have supplied our burner and kept the living room cosy all winter. It's the way that their small saw-toothed pinnate leaves – cotton soft when fresh in May – permit sunlight to pierce down to the ground and allow the flowers to grow at their feet. I also love their rich gift of place names – Ashbourne, Ashford, Monyash, Ashwood – to the folk of Derbyshire.

Their ability to grow from bare limestone seems itself like a kind of giving. On the slopes between Monsal and Cressbrook there are patches of naked scree where nothing else can gain a foothold. The sheep steer clear and in the absence of those grinding molars the ash saplings bite down into the rock and take ground that nothing else uses. On the railway cuttings on the opposite side, near the old Monsal Station, ash saplings follow the undulating creases in the sheer limestone. Under their joint instincts for light and water, thousands of ash force down a taproot into the horizontal seam and then turn through a sharp 90-degree angle, firing bolt upright towards the heavens. If one could see with X-ray vision the full extent of each one, top to toe, they would all be perfectly L-shaped.

If ash is generous, it is also tough and niggardly. The young ones are striplings of whip wood, iron grey and smooth with a texture that reminds me of russet apples. The base is often orange stained, the buds are black and shaped like tiny hooves. Each lost twig along the stem marks its short life with a curved thorn-like snag cut deep into the bark. Yet as the trunk grows the stretch marks along its boll deepen and widen into coarse fissures; the limbs unfold with the quality of antlers, opening themselves wide to the mean winter light of Derbyshire.

25 February 2008

CLAXTON

To call it a valley or even a vale would be misleading. It is a fold in the landscape, whose central crease is marked by a narrow meander of slow-moving water that we know as Carleton Beck. By the time I arrived the mist, which must have lingered all morning, had faded to the merest ghost just distinct enough to take the ochre edge off the reedbed. Through its faded colours drifted a barn owl hunting by daylight, a not uncommon occurrence at this time of year.

In the Yare Valley we are particularly blessed with the species, and sightings are often a daily, or nightly, event. Within eight kilometres of this spot I know three churches that have housed them and two neighbours each with occupied nestboxes. This year we are planning a census of the breeding population in the neighbouring few parishes.

The owl ploughed a wandering course around the bushes and then even, for a short while, it hunted through the alder wood, where I could follow its course intermittently – a buff realm of intention and silent movement through the stark and dead-coloured chaos of the winter trees. And then it did something startling. It stopped and went to sleep. At first I didn't know this.

When it perched I played a game to get as close as possible. I aligned myself with an alder and then walked closer and closer, thinking it would fly at any minute. When I'd covered the length of the field and reached the fence, I realised how I had done it. The bird was perched, slumped to one side, the head tilted down. The heart-shaped facial disk was a crumpled triangle and its eye a diagonal dark slit. Once, momentarily, this crevice parted, just enough to suggest an owl's dreams, then it closed again. As I walked away leaving an owl asleep in the woods it felt like a privilege and an achievement all in one.

26 February 2007

LYNFORD, NORFOLK

A friend of mine put it best: he said winter lasted about six hours where he lived. Some ancient, rustic-edged voice deep within me keeps saying that at some point we're going to have to pay for it all, but for now I'm relishing the moment. At Lynford arboretum spring wasn't so much on its way: it was in full residence with the windows and doors flung wide open. There were twelve bird species 'singing' (including a great spotted woodpecker's pneumatic drill), which is a chorus more typical of late March than February.

The song thrushes were the undoubted stars. The cleverly blended mix of open turf and widely spaced mature trees at this site is clearly song thrush heaven. Male birds seemed to be present every few metres and were busy staking out their small patch with a palisade of music. One particular contest between immediate neighbours had progressed far beyond defence into outright attack, with the two producing streams of rattle notes that had the intensity of gunfire.

It was interesting to contrast these song wars with the performance of a close relative. A mistle thrush always seems to maintain an aura of serene aloofness. It is partly a function of the bird singing from the crown of a tree and therefore physically way above the others, and partly a function of the sound itself, which has a far-off meditative quality.

The mistle thrush's song is also a perfect analogue for the species' mode of flight. When airborne it intersperses each burst of wing strokes with a long and slightly downward glide. As a consequence the bird seems to roll across the sky. The song, meanwhile, has a similar and slowly waving structure. At Lynford the missie sent out these long, sinuous curves of sound that acted as weft for the song thrushes' exuberant howitzer notes, and together the two birds enmeshed the entire landscape in an impermeable sense of hope.

27 February 2006

CLAXTON

Whenever I reach for the wellingtons and binoculars I could walk in any direction from my house and find wildlife. Yet something hardwired into my brain means that my internal compass always trends to the north, down to the River Yare, which makes its sluggish meandering course to the sea just a short distance away. What is it about the river that always draws me back, rather than any other land feature in the parish?

The answer may well lie about three metres beneath my neighbours' garden. Several years ago they found a mysterious object in the deep, black, peaty soil and after several days' excavation discovered what was probably the remains of an ancient boat. Stone Age people were almost certainly drawn to this place – which was then on the edge of a great tidal estuary – in search of what ecologists call ecotones.

They are the border areas between two distinct habitats. Woodland edge is a classic ecotone. Coastal strips and riverbanks – those often indeterminate margins between land and water – are two more. They were attractive to humans precisely because they are often the richest point in any landscape for wildlife. Some of the strongest evidence of Neolithic diets comes from the great middens of shells and refuse where people processed the rich pickings from their daily trawl of such border areas. I sometimes wonder if the inexhaustible fascination that children have for poking in rock pools and tidal shallows is a reflection of this same ancient impulse.

Just as Neolithic foragers were drawn to boat along these margins, so is the modern naturalist enticed to the same space. While I trawl for words and they sought shells, fish or fowl, we are both making the same intrinsic hunter-gatherer's choice. So don't ask why I go down to the river. I'm simply doing what my Stone Age forebears told me to do.

MARCH

8 March 2010

HADDISCOE, NORFOLK

At last! The light finally flared down upon these expansive flats with all its customary winter dazzle. Far off the mobs of rooks were turned silver in the sunshine and as they descended en masse they looked like scrapyard metal clattering onto the fields. For the first time this year I also heard a sound I've longed to hear. Lapwings breed still in good numbers and, although I'm well aware of their catastrophic losses Europe-wide (half gone in the last thirty years), this wonderful place gives me the illusion that all is well with the world. And now they're singing.

Lapwings are compelling even in normal flight. The broad, floppy, rounded wings seem to have too much surface for the bird's weight. It is as if excess of lift makes lapwings unstable and intermittently they have to tilt sideways, spilling the accumulated air out like a valve to release pressure. Yet during display, lapwing flight is glossed purple with an insane perfection. The males mount up the vertical walls of spring light, hold momentarily and tumble down the other side, then twist and rock crazily over the Earth before repeating it all again. The whole time they let fly with that wild heart-piercing song, which, this year, is more piercing than ever. Death entered our lives this winter and I think of our beloved friend, with whom I once walked these marshes and who will never hear lapwings again. A common response towards all of nature is to assume that the bird itself is filled with some of the feelings of joy that its performance inspires. I don't believe that or, at least, I feel we can never know what it feels. Yet there is in its behaviour a kind of joy – or would we be better to call it a kind of love? – that is rooted in it being only and perfectly itself. It is our encounter with this absoluteness in the natural world that heals us but which, as a society, we have yet to value truly or find a means to harness fully.

12 March 2007

CLAXTON

In our parish I usually know whenever a female sparrowhawk is passing overhead because she triggers a boiling clamour of rook calls and jackdaw notes across the marsh, followed moments later by an aimless wake of fear flights involving all those birds that are her potential victims. I would love to know the total calorific cost of these dread-filled responses; but then imagine that full energy bill generated over the lifetime of a single major predator. My guess is that the calories expended by all the escapees far exceeds the amount consumed by the hawk herself in the form of the ensnared and plucked bodies that never made a clean getaway.

The other part of the relationship that never ceases to amaze me is the speed with which the rooks spot her. Often I would never see the hawk at all except the corvids had already picked out her tiny silhouette. Today, instead of watching the sparrowhawk through binoculars, I tried to use my naked eye the better to appreciate the rooks' own powers of sight. Alas, she was little more than a gnat-sized speck across the faceless sky, a floater sliding down my cornea. The other thing you can surmise is that sparrowhawks (and rooks) have no floaters and certainly don't suffer the kind of myopia I have. The short-sighted raptor is one of those weird flowers that blooms for one day only.

Finally, I try to imagine what it is to see the world through a hawk's eyes. Is it the same world as the one I see, only more crystalline and more precise? Or is it something altogether different? In his book *The Peregrine*, J. A. Baker imagined that the raptor in flight inhabited a molten world where the Earth's fixed properties liquefy and assume the character of a lava-like stream of tones and shadows. 'Pouring away behind the moving bird,' Baker wrote, 'the land flows out from the eye in deltas of piercing colour.'

13 March 2006

CARLETON ST PETER, NORFOLK

Jackdaws are surely one of our most sociable birds. The poet Kathleen Jamie perfectly caught their easy companionability when she described them side by side like pairs of old shoes. The jackdaw singleton is virtually an oxymoron, but occasionally I spot one flying overhead, when the bird's ceaseless barrage of contact notes seems like an attempt to reassure itself of imminent company.

With the recent rise in temperature a small flock mills daily around Carleton's isolated church and not even a constant downpour can reduce the birds' high spirits. They glide upwards in spirals over the tower, while their calls ring out sharply like someone striking together two pieces of flint. One wonders if the resonant lapidary qualities to their vocalisations, which are caught in both syllables of the onomatopoeic name, have evolved as a consequence of the species' long association with rock faces and sea cliffs. The huge planes of stone serve as a resonating chamber for their flint-knapped calls and double the frequency by bouncing back an echo of each note.

Jackdaws have found a ready alternative to the natural cliff face in the towering walls of stone that we prefer to think of as churches and cathedrals. Throw in a little neglect, which leaves the building riddled with the sort of niches that make perfect nest sites, and you can understand why the jackdaw is also the most religious of our birds. In Norfolk, the birds' flinty calls and flint stones perform a kind of ecclesiastical double act, because there is hardly a church in the county where both are not embedded in the tower. In turn, they are as integral to our sense of the region's identity as that other wonderfully atmospheric inhabitant of our religious architecture called *Xanthoria parietina*. You'll know this routine churchgoer better as the lichen that spreads its yolk-yellow rosettes upon the gravestones, like a natural memorial to the departed souls.

19 March 2012

CLAXTON

Our rook-winged weathervane indicates south-westerlies but I suspect the arrow has not moved for days. The air is cold but utterly still and the grey overhead is fathomless so that the dullest light makes the swans on the marsh look like matt-white cavities in a flat plane of dead sedge. Yet it's the sheer flatness of this atmosphere that somehow makes the hunting short-eared owls seem all the more intensely alive.

They've been here for weeks, up to three, and always at least one hunting by daylight. The plumage is a classic predator's earth tone disrupted by darker chequering, while along the wings are crescentic patches of black and ginger. The wings are as broad as a barn owl's but they are longer and it gives to the bird's flight a more languid fluency. It almost has a slow-motion quality, with more back-lift than down-stroke – an even, pulsing, hunter's metronome. Yet it acquires a brief inelegance whenever the owl bothers to take in my presence. As it flies its staring yellow eyes fix me, the angle of the face turning ever more awkwardly, until the tension finally releases and the head returns to the bird's own plough line. Every now and then the owl plunges for prey, and those long wings suddenly collapse like a piece of damp clothing dropped to the ground. For the few moments that the creature remains earthbound I can take in the great cat's head and the huge cat's eyes. Then up it rises once again.

Recently two owls have interacted, as if to signal the first green flush of hormone that will eventually drive them back to the upland moors to breed. In these sparring moments the owls utter a strange call. It is breathy and hard, suggestive even of pain and somewhat like a gull's brief cry. Yet, in truth, no words can quite get it. It's a sound before language – a raw simple poem about life and need.

22 March 2009

CLAXTON

Decoy Carr is a flooded patch of coppiced alder near our house that probably dates to Roman times. It is so overgrown it would fulfil most people's ideas of jungle and even I breathe easier once I've broken back out. Perhaps we find woods like this troubling and claustrophobic because they resist us linguistically as much as they bar and impede us physically. They are so complex in terms of texture, colour and form that we feel entangled in mind as well as in body. There is just so much that is unspoken and even unspeakable about woods. We often cut and clear them to access their underlying fertility, but perhaps it is also a way of freeing ourselves from their unconscious demands.

Recently I told myself that I was going down daily to look for woodcock; or even for the newly discovered pleasure of fungi, such as scarlet elf cup that spangles the place in buttons of crimson plastic. But perhaps what I'm really hunting for is words. The most resistant is a great citadel of greens across the woodland floor. The colour context for them is a brittle frame of sedge-coloured stems that was last year's nettle bank, and which has now flopped over everywhere rather like brushed hair. Through this is a meandering tracery of deer paths where narrow hooves, mingling brown with green, have driven down into the muck fragments of moss and leaves.

Around this network are open stretches dominated by three shades. There is the intense yellow-green of moss that plates an industrial-like entanglement of sallow branches, which, in turn, pipe this colour everywhere above the leaf litter. Then there is the pure grass green of new nettles pushing through. Finally and most compelling is a deep shining emerald where lords and ladies has bulged out from the dead matter lying on the black humus, a green colour that is bold and even vulgar with its easy sense of new life.

22 March 2010

CLAXTON

What is it about brimstones that moves us so much? Already I've had three emails from friends telling me of their first for the year. One neighbour even intimated that the sight of this butterfly brought spring to their lane. I feel it has much to do with the landscape at the moment that brimstones first emerge. It is a curious time because, despite all those promising gestures of new life, the countryside is exhausted by March. In the Derbyshire of my childhood I always felt that the cold had burnt the hills to a soft dead-straw tone. The same occurs in Norfolk, but the month's dominant colour is blended with the dead pale copper of old oak leaves.

A further aspect here is that the landscape actually seems to shrink. March is that point when the paths finally dry out and you can exchange wellingtons for leather boots. In that loss of excess water the whole place seems to slump and contract even more and, when you add in those winter-wasted pale colours, you have a kind of final deadness to the countryside. It is into this very specific atmosphere that a brimstone makes its deeply moving entrance.

Yellow is, of course, already present by this stage. There is, for instance, a glorious yellow lichen, especially on the elders at the end of the lane. In the sunshine it looks about the same tone as the yolks in free-range eggs. There is also a kind of yellowish sheen to moss in certain lights. Then there is the pink yellow that comes through in the beak of a heron as the breeding season approaches. All of these are pleasing on the eye but the sight of that male brimstone, that wide swoop of lemon yellow, which seems so filled with a sense of adventure as it sails across the fields, is more than a colour. It is a song of hope that stirs the very heart.

24 March 2008

Claxton

For the first time ever the porcelain-white heron with wire-thin legs and serpentine neck called the little egret has arrived in strength on our marsh. There were five today, seven yesterday, probing the fringes to the pools, patrolling ditches and shuttling back and forth across the river.

It is odd to recall that in 1974 I drove to see one in Lancashire when it was a rarity. By 1990 egrets began to spread across southern English wetlands. Now they're routine in Norfolk, breeding and settling into many parts as if they had always been there. Yet this is the first time they have graced our patch and it feels as strange and new as that first sighting thirty-four years ago.

I've quickly learnt to separate the creamy white of the swans from the immaculate frost-white of the egrets. I've learnt to watch for the rhythmic snaking jerk of its S-shaped neck – a signature movement almost – which accompanies each precision pace of an egret. I've noticed too how this, in turn, has made the heron's comparable forward thrust as it prowls along the dykes now seem coarse by comparison.

As I adapt to this new, subtle register of sights and experiences that the egret's arrival has enforced I wonder if the other creatures have to make a similar adjustment. Do the neighbouring waterbirds have to acquire the same subliminal recognition of egret white and egret kinetics in order to know that all is well on the marsh?

I wonder equally about the otter whose black fish-odoured spraint stains the path and who, tonight, may well mark my passage as I now note his. Will that otter wonder at the flavour of egret? What will it make of that dazzling burst of white when it disturbs its first egret upon the dyke? You imagine that this vast concatenation of adjustments involving all the residents of our marsh will have to be made before an egret can truly feel that this is home.

26 March 2005

HORSEY BROAD, NORFOLK

This spot is about the most easterly point in Britain, and it was intriguing to reflect that northwards there was nothing except sea all the way to the Arctic Ocean. As we scanned across the huge expanse of ploughland it definitely felt as if we were at an edge; in fact, on the edge of several intersecting frontiers.

One was occupied by a flock of starlings that sleeted constantly back and forth. The decision to land by the vanguard caused them all to heap up in one dark pool, from which arose that wonderful rash of burbling noises that is always an accompaniment to starlings en masse. Several fieldfares bounded among them adding a dash of bright colour – their blue-grey crowns and rich ochreous chests splattered with black – and a flock of golden plovers kept up their beautiful soft whistling calls.

Whenever the electric fizz of the starlings waned, the plovers' gentle rhythmic undertow of sound came through.

All these birds are migrants and poised at Britain's periphery for a final leap back to Europe. We could easily imagine how the tableau unfolding here was being re-enacted along the entire coast – an assembly and eventual exodus involving millions of birds. Just as we had caught the spatial frontier for this massive outpouring, so we touched the edge of another drama, this one temporal and sexual. All around male lapwings corkscrewed wildly upwards in preposterous self-advertisement, while a female marsh harrier, celebrating her own prowess, rode drunkenly up and down the sky in long, exaggerated strokes. Only the day before a mutual friend had expressed it thus: 'It's opening time in nature's great saloon.'

27 March 2006

ROCKLAND BROAD, NORFOLK

Perhaps it was the stink of fox snaking a parallel course down the track that made me hope it was a day for predators. Yet initially their presence was implied rather than directly evident. I had one exciting moment when a wave of songbird alarm calls ran through the waterside alders like a shiver, but I could find nothing that might have triggered it. A similar experience occurred as I trained my telescope on a great crested grebe. The recently acquired corolla of chestnut feathers around the bird's crown suddenly slicked down and the whole body was pressed to the water as if it were smothering its own shadow. What had its brilliant red eyes spotted that I couldn't?

It was an hour before I got my answer. Marsh harriers are often easy to pick out even at range, because it's about the only local bird that flies without a flap for long periods. A lingering airborne stillness suddenly drew my eye high overhead to the speck centred in a vast dark cavern of rain cloud. There were two marsh harriers circling at huge range – perhaps a kilometre high – but the third bird with them was a peregrine. Its distinctive anchor silhouette twisted in tight spirals close to one of the harriers and it was obvious that there was some electric pulse of emotion between them. Suddenly the game of aerial tag spilled into something far more dramatic. Briefly the two birds locked talons and fell earthwards before swooping away and resuming their parallel maneouvres. They then cruised across the heavens, dust motes tracking west, until they were momentarily fixed against the flaring whiteness of sunlit cloud.

As the three remarkable birds patrolled those deep canyons of cold air I began to wonder above which unlikely places are such scenes played out that go entirely undetected by their terrestrial neighbours? How often do we plod the Earth oblivious of the drama lost overhead in that vast pale eye of secrecy?

29 March 2004

CLAXTON

Come high wind or spring sunshine the vocal duel between two local song thrushes wakes me every morning at the moment. I like to visualise those gutsy, clanging, joyous notes pouring out like freshly tempered shards of steel, the hot sparks flying wildly as they spin through the air. Song thrushes produce a sound with the power to batter rivets into winter's coffin, to force the buds to open or to wake a hedgehog instantly from its hibernation. It is a fabulous noise that gains momentum as the season draws on, with a vocalist adding new motifs to his repertoire. A bird borrows elements from the others that it can hear, and you can imagine these scraps of melody being passed all around the country as one song thrush tosses the sound-torch to its song thrush neighbour.

In his book *The Charm of Birds* Viscount Grey of Fallodon wrote that if a vocalist 'were to be regarded as endeavouring to please us by song, the thrush should be put first among British birds'. In a recent RSPB poll that is exactly what happened: we voted it the No. 1 species for its song of joy. Yet how strange that in another recent study published in *Science*, the authors showed that the most accurate data we have on wildlife populations indicate across-the-board declines. The thrush is typical. The British Trust for Ornithology discovered that half of them have gone in thirty years. Why are we so complacent about our loss of wildlife? What price should we put on the song thrush's priceless song? How dare we not make that song a political issue? Yet I doubt the subject of regional wildlife extinction in Britain will even be mentioned at the forthcoming general election.

APRIL

2 April 2013

Thetford, Norfolk

'If you don't see it you can have my Land Rover!' reassured my friend David Tipling as we walked upstream from the town centre. It's the sort of guarantee you want as you go in search of one of the country's most elusive animals. Sure enough, as predicted, the young male otter, completely wild but long habituated to humans, swam nonchalantly upstream.

The creature's approach may have been meandering and leisured, but our responses were anything but: photographers and other observers rushed to take positions, often lying on hail-soaked ground, or making final adjustments to equipment. Some cameras were sunk on tripods into the current at an otter's-eye level and when the beast rose out of the River Thet to sniff at a mossy knoll the camera shutters volleyed like machine-gun rounds.

If the otter glanced edgily at its paparazzi reception it was on terms of absolute amity with the water. I noticed that as it emerged the stream had left long linear current lines through its fur so that the whole creature had a graphic quality, as if the Thet had actually drawn it. When the otter dived back under, the action was less a manoeuvre foisted by a living creature upon its inanimate surroundings. It had an air of collaboration. As much as the otter plunged, the water yielded. There was no splash. It was like a quick shot of oil fired into the stream's laminar pulse. They blended and off it swam to porpoise and plunge for ninety more magical minutes. It rootled in rafts of riverbank vegetation, it surfaced with pencil-thin elvers or tiddlers called bullheads, whose olive scales were shot through with notes of orange and lime; at one turbid mass it burrowed under and bulked up sloughs of weed so that the violent twist and bulge of vegetation clothed the otter's every move. Nothing held it for more than moments. Always, as it went, we could follow the submerged line of its course by the champagne effervescence of otter breath, rising back into this plodding world where we had simply to stand and watch.

4 April 2011

CLAXTON

Spring came to me this morning in one of its stranger but also perhaps more sensuous guises. I lifted the lid on our compost bin and there were several hundred earthworms wound almost continuously around the lid. It was as if the warm dank rotting mass in the bin – the fractured eggshells and papery outer leaves of leeks and the oozy black skins of bananas – had exhaled all that richly squirming life for the first time this year. Judging from the number of segments in their tubular bodies (under the microscope I made counts of 116 and 110) they belong to a species that goes by the name of the brandling worm. I suspect also that they are taking time out from their sumptuous diet to breed and, as they writhed in unison, they inscribed slow-moving purple-pink hieroglyphs against the black plastic.

Other earthworms have already made a mark on my sense of season, if a little more subliminally. Charles Darwin, himself a great devotee of these humble creatures, estimated that the cumulative worm casts produced by the population in each acre amounted to about 16 tonnes of shifted soil a year. While the rain washes some of the soil nutrients and minerals downwards, the worms mine these buried stores and carry them back to the surface. So the first stands of red dead nettle and lesser celandine along the Claxton paths owe some of their April colour to the work of worms.

Another way in which the creatures have unconsciously staked their place in my sense of moment is in the bulging pouch, suspended below the bone-white beaks of our breeding rooks. The birds feed constantly on earthworms, and young rooks are merely raucous black transmutations of worm. Since I once ate rook pie I have, I suppose, eaten worms myself. However, the form in which I love them most is the heady soft meditations that rise at dawn like mist from the throats of our local blackbirds.

5 April 2010

Staverton, Suffolk

This wonderful hunting park dates to the thirteenth century and apparently still holds four thousand ancient oaks, many of them more than four hundred years old. Although it is adjacent to the road, the area known as The Thicks is perhaps the most atmospheric. As its name suggests, it is dense and dark, a mood imposed mainly by some of the oldest holly trees found anywhere in Britain. Constantly one has to duck down below the deer browse-line in order to struggle through.

The combination of these two dominant tree species creates an intriguing tension at Staverton. Aside from the far more abundant ivy, I don't think any plant species creates more greenery in winter than holly. The presence of such trees in any landscape instils in us that sense of an imperishable part of life continuing irrespective of season. Oaks, however, have the opposite effect in early spring. With the exception of the ash, perhaps no tree clings more to a sense of winter than the oak. The trees are reluctant not just to leaf but to yield any notion that life will ever return to their grave and silent branches. So

The Thicks were truly thick with a sense of life and dense with an air of death.

In a curious reversal of my expectations, it was the latter that created much of Staverton's glorious otherness. Bizarre, withered oak trunks, hewn back by time to mere totem poles of rot, continued their defiance of gravity perhaps a century after they first ceased to live. Other collapsed giants, yielding steadily to fungus over the decades, somehow managed to rise up off their elbows out of the leaf litter and send out wonderfully grainy bare branches that carried the eye into the next section of wood. Then you'd come upon some still-standing, still-living veteran, its heartwood eaten away entirely, yet around its vast hollowed-out bulk there is even now a calloused façade deeply suggestive of an immense and heroic life.

6 April 2009

CLAXTON

The latest addition to the spring chorus is a rather strange song, but it is no less welcome for that. It is also a microscopic sound. In fact, I heard it last week but then it had only registered subliminally. When I finally identified it, there was a simultaneous moment of realisation: it had been calling to me now for days.

The song is simple as well as small – like a thumb rubbing briefly on rubber, or the coarse honk of a greylag goose, but reduced to a fragment and sounding as if it has travelled from way across the far fields. Yet it isn't so distant. It is coming from the dyke by the path. Its author, hanging at the surface, limbs slackly dangled and spreadeagled, looks like a newborn baby immersed in water. The male toad sculls towards me and clambers on to some floating vegetation. In the sun the swollen tubercles of his upper body dry to the colour of an old cowpat. His eyelids half close, reducing the irises to black slits and the eyes themselves to copper bulges of sleepy contentment.

Occasionally he wakes and lets rip with his croak and it is odd to hear this 350-million-year-old song, as ancient as the Carboniferous, mingling with the buzzy fart of a plane overhead. That noise means nothing to my toad, but when further down the dyke there comes a tiny chirp of opposition he rouses himself to face the vocal challenge. His bulk is raised up the better to project his voice, and he assumes a posture that looks one half sphinx, one half mud fist. The whole body balloons out and quickly sucks down, simultaneously causing the neck to bellow outwards. The mouth never opens and his new-moon smile remains clamped to his face, yet from within that white throat, with its black flecks and granule-like rugosities, there comes a miniature song that tells of wet and warmth and warts and sex.

7 April 2008

Buxton, Derbyshire

A male blackbird gave its hard tin-plate clatter as I approached and then made one of those long arrow-straight dives for the darkest part of the wood. It was such a dull morning and so gloomy under the trees that the brightest thing I saw all day was that crocus-yellow bill.

I stopped by a large pool to look for frogs. There were none to be seen, not even lurking in the deepest part of the water. Yet at one edge of the pond there were abundant signs of their earlier presence. A great floating slobber of spawn lolled in the shallows. It was so vast and dense it seemed as if there was too much for the depth of the pond and the uppermost cells had been forced above the waterline. Frost had got hold of this top layer and the skin looked crinkled and dehydrated.

In one place a hard white crust had formed and the aqueous jelly inside several cells of spawn had expanded and burst apart like pustules. All around this unhealthy swelling, I noticed that the normally black eggs within the sacs had gone white. They didn't so much look dead; it was as if the last signs of lifelessness were already dissolving away, like almost-melted specks of hail. Just below the water's surface, however, the eggs had already started to change form and if not tadpole-shaped, and if still entirely motionless, they were at least in the midst of that great becoming.

I noticed how deeper into the life-giving pond, about 15 centimetres down, and at the edges of the solid mass, the spawn cells had a perfect globular structure. They swayed slightly as the breeze worked across the water, reminding me briefly of other times and jam jars and spring sunshine. But deeper still, almost on the muddy bottom, the stuff had acquired a strange and captivating ambiguity, like brown clouds across a bitter black sky.

9 April 2007

CLAXTON

It was so bright it could have been a flower at my feet. It was a rook's eggshell – a delicate green-blue wash overlain with brown markings that are sparse at the broad 'top' but which intensify into a wildly random mess of squiggles and blotches at the narrow end. To the eye the whole shell had a silky sheen and was perfectly smooth, but I was surprised to see that under a hand-lens the egg's surface was pitted and irregular, like well-worn marble.

The secret inner life of my egg led to reflections on the many curious but momentous links between the microscopic and the everyday world. One such became apparent in the fifties when the peregrine, the world's fastest flying organism, mysteriously plummeted in numbers. It was eventually proved that DDT, a chemical once heralded as an agricultural cure-all, was causing the bird to lay unnaturally thin-shelled eggs. These were breaking in the normal process of incubation and the species' breeding success collapsed, particularly in parts of Europe and America. The difference between survival and extinction may have rested on half a millimetre of calcium in the egg wall.

There were other reflections inside my egg. For instance, those shells with wonderfully unpredictable patterns are coloured as the egg travels along the oviduct inside the mother, where it picks up minute, random dribbles of bile or blood. Each egg is completely unique – and it's these unrepeated, chance colours that set the egg collector's pulse racing. Recently one of the most notorious fell from a tree while practising his dark art and died. It's odd to think that he lost his life for a few micrograms of a bird's body fluids.

Meanwhile, I can tell that the former occupant of my egg is elsewhere, on that momentous stage of its young life in the treetops. I can hear its helium voice – a minuscule squeak like the sound of rubber moved between two fingers. In this northerly-lashed landscape it's almost all I have to remind me of spring.

10 April 2006

Boscastle, Cornwall

In this beautiful, ancient landscape, nothing impressed me more than the country lane that meanders past Minster church, lying in the steep-sided vale of a tributary for the River Valency. Although it is now tarmacked, the single-lane track, known as a holloway, may be thousands of years old and it was mesmerising to think how many people must have passed this same way.

Gradually all the plodding feet and trampling hooves worked in concert with the rain to scour out an ever-deepening crease into the earth. In places the steep banks rise up three to four metres, and the hedgerow trees that grow out of their tops often link arms above the middle of the lane to create a glorious tunnel of vegetation. Wherever a rotten stump has been ripped out of the bank, the resulting cavity allows one to glimpse its internal construction. Many are filled with stone, then topped with a skin of soil. At certain points, where the bank had once collapsed onto the lane, unseen hands rebuilt the sides, often creating beautiful herringbone patterns out of the slate slabs.

These sheer faces are now wonderful rock gardens smothered in golden saxifrage, lesser celandine, wood anemone, pennywort, primrose and dog's mercury. Others bristle with hard fern, hart's tongue and rippling skirts of ivy. In one bank a near-vertical carpet of luminous green moss cascades down the rock face. One can also see where badgers have carved their own thoroughfare into the landscape, spurning the human route.

Wandering along this magnificent holloway, where the overwhelming effects of rain and photosynthesis make it seem as if the light itself is saturated in green, I found myself reflecting on how creative the relationship can be between humans and the rest of nature, particularly if we take things together one slow step at a time.

20 April 2009

LONGNOR, STAFFORDSHIRE

Our usual routine while watching this badgers' sett is to sit on the hillside opposite, about 30 metres from the action. However, we agreed by various silent gestures to attempt to get closer. A breeze was blowing straight across the sett and down the line of an adjacent wall. So, screened by this, we crept upwind and stopped eventually, incredulous that the badgers still couldn't see us. In fact, one proceeded down the wall almost underneath us and so close that we could detect the red clay smudges on his white blaze and the sharp inward breath as he paused to snout and grub for worms. We waited as he walked away and knew at some point that the angle of the wind would bring a badger's super-sense into play. Who knows what microscopic part of vaporised human fatty acids carried from us to him, but sure enough he came dashing back to the sett still oblivious of our exact location, but absolutely certain that he could smell the presence of potential danger.

We assumed this comic moment was all we would see of them, but his partner had remained grooming at the sett. Her untroubled demeanour must have reassured him because, as we casually started to walk away from the spot, we suddenly realised they were all still there. Separated by just 3 metres of April gloom, we watched this badger pair enfolded as a warm, supple ball of pied stripes, he scratching and nibbling her flea-tormented pelt as passionately as she did herself. She reclined, her stub tail standing proud like a shaving brush, while he nuzzled her sexual parts and all around her swollen teats.

So much intimacy at such close range brought its own peculiar kind of tension. It was a glorious privilege but mingled with it was an uneasy feeling of deception. Had they not finally sensed that their mutual affection was not as private as it ought to have been, I think we would probably have whispered across to them – species to species, so to speak – to resume more normal relations.

21 April 2008

Claxton

My computer program for handling digital images allows me to enlarge my photograph of a moth until it is fifteen times its life size. At that scale the two-centimetre insect, caught the other day in my moth trap, is anything but the image conjured by its name. The clouded drab is really rather beautiful. Its forewings are rich deep chestnut and down the length of each of these runs a series of darker veins, intersected by a pale cross-line. On the forewing's leading edge are two kidney-shaped stigmata outlined faintly in white. At this scale a clouded drab is also arresting for other reasons. I must confess that the down-turned antennae resemble a rodent's wiry tail and the thickly furred 'shoulders' give its thorax an unsettling, almost mammalian bulk.

However, I am captivated most when I reflect upon what seems the miraculous transformations undertaken by this commonplace insect. Think, for instance, that last spring it was a dome-shaped egg on the underside of hawthorn or sallow leaves. By summer it evolved as a caterpillar of bluish green with crisp longitudinal lines of white and black. In autumn it became a chrysalis like a dark brown pill. It emerged as an adult last year, but hibernated as the creature I see on my computer screen and then awoke this month to settle in my trap.

This is one metamorphosis, but the second and possibly more intriguing transformation is the one allowing it to reach you. While we think of a digital camera, computer, the internet and the pages of a book as all intrinsically human and artificial, might they also be part of that inexorable machinery we call natural selection? By making this further journey beyond its usual habitat and through our cultural world as a thing of beauty and significance, does this insect gain a tiny selective advantage? By touching and moving the human imagination, has a clouded drab made its world a slightly more favourable place for its continued survival?

23 April 2005

EDINBURGH

It was a treat recently to view the painting by Raphael entitled *The Madonna of the Pinks,* when it was briefly on display in Edinburgh at the Scottish National Gallery. Not only does this exquisite A4-sized work have an intriguing allegorical content, but it has also enjoyed an extraordinary history. For much of its life in England the painting was unrecognised as truly the work of Raphael and was locked away at Alnwick Castle, the home of the Dukes of Northumberland. Its real significance was not appreciated until 1991 and almost immediately it looked set to depart after the Getty Museum in California had offered to buy it for a staggering thirty-five million pounds. At the eleventh hour the National Gallery prevented its export and bought it with help from a record Heritage Lottery grant of £11.5 million.

In Edinburgh *The Madonna of the Pinks* was accompanied by a range of medieval and Renaissance paintings that were intended to demonstrate the evolution in artistic treatment of Mother Mary with the Holy Child. One image by Bernardo Daddi (dated *c.*1350) is representative of about five hundred similar paintings of Christ that include the image of a goldfinch. In fact, Raphael painted just such a work entitled *Madonna del Cardellino.*

Early religious writers often incorporated animals into the Christian story and the goldfinch's crimson face patch and thistle-feeding habits had long prompted associations with the blood and thorn crown of the crucifixion. But it was also a bird symbolic of light and fertility, so its appearance in a painting of the Madonna and child was intended to conjure both the dark fate awaiting the infant Jesus and also the promise of redemption that his adult life offered to us all. Although these resonances are lost today it is assumed that they would have been picked up by Raphael's own sixteenth-century audience.

In *The Madonna of the Pinks* Raphael employed a similar method to convey his message. While there is something remarkably natural in the way the young Jesus fingers the beautiful little blooms just handed to him by his mother, the flowers were also chosen for their symbolism. Wild dianthus or carnations were imbued with ideas of devotional love and marriage so, in passing them to her son, Mary was making a commitment not only as his mother but as the Bride of Christ.

Flowers still retain a powerful symbolism – think of the romantic associations attaching to roses – and at this time of year how many of us have expressed affection or simply celebrated the arrival of spring with a bunch of daffodils? But while the core message might survive, the subtler pattern to our floral language has been lost. And what has undoubtedly gone from our lives is the opportunity to express ourselves with wild flowers. Don't misunderstand me, I'm not at all advocating anyone should revive the lost custom by harvesting armfuls of wild bluebells or early purple orchids. But shouldn't we consider it sad that in our hands-off age of environmental impoverishment, wild flowers are now far too scarce and precious for us to enjoy the luxury of picking a few?

The habit has been lost in my relatively short lifetime because I can distinctly recall how, in the 1960s, my brother and sisters and I used to gather flowers for our mother. I was going to suggest that they were usually no more than a bunch of buttercups, but now you would be hard pressed even to find a Derbyshire buttercup meadow as profusely yellow as the one near our home. In Norfolk today that same golden vision from my childhood is largely confined to the nature reserve.

Among the handful of buttercups we would often add something a bit more special, like the delicate mauve of a cuckooflower, or – dare I tell you – the magenta of the occasional marsh orchid. Fortunately the flowers still grow in the damp patch by my parents' house and it is a measure of how quickly attitudes change that I can recall the jolt of mental electricity when, some years ago, I entered a restaurant in Greece where each table was decorated with a tiny pot of wild orchids. Even then I was struck by the deep irony. In Britain we have come to hold dear what we have largely destroyed, but in large parts of Greece they still have a sufficient profusion of wild flowers to take a few of them for granted.

Viewing *The Madonna of the Pinks* allowed me to reflect that the decline of our commonest wildlife involves a severe cultural toll as well as the more obvious ecological price. I suspect that today the humble daisy or the sticky-stemmed dandelion represents the last opportunity for our children to express themselves with a gift of wild flowers. Should we ever lose it completely then we will have surrendered a fundamental and shared appreciation of natural beauty and diminished our language of affection and exchange. Now that truly seems a high price to pay.

23 April 2007

CLAXTON

A broken pantile in the roof above my office means that each spring a pair of starlings uses it as a nest hole. As I write I can see the parents arrow in with beakfuls of insects, and the gift seems to arouse pleasure among the nest occupants, because amid the squawking and shuffle of bodies the male begins a quiet subsong. His usual jangle of clucking, whistles and fizzing sounds is interspersed with note-perfect imitations of curlew, chicken and tawny owl sounds. It has the effect of compressing a whole host of other landscapes and seasons into our shared living space.

Starlings are one of about ten British species that routinely copy the vocalisations of other birds, but perhaps the most unlikely mimic is the bullfinch. Its own song is a quiet introverted piping, but for centuries birdkeepers were aware that young bullfinches could be taught to produce a whole host of other sounds. In Hardy's *Tess of the D'Urbervilles,* the heroine is put to work training the birds. Some individuals were even trained to sing whole tunes such as 'God Save the Queen' (alas, not the Sex Pistols' version) and 'Rule Britannia'.

One tale I cherish, which is so far-fetched it might just be true, concerned a Victorian musician who lost a valuable flute, which was defective because of a loss of pitch on one of the upper notes. Suspicions for its theft first fell on a charwoman but she was proved innocent when the musician happened to visit a friend's house some months later. The host had recently bought a bullfinch and it had been taught to copy an instrument and sing several tunes beautifully, except that it skipped certain notes each time. The musician reflected that the bullfinch's omissions tallied precisely with the false notes on his own lost flute. When he confronted his erstwhile friend with the instrument's theft, the latter broke down and confessed to the crime.

26 April 2004

LONGNOR, STAFFORDSHIRE

The first badger to appear trundled to the mouth of its hole and stared briefly in our direction, then with a hard sniff at the cold air it got down to the opening chore of the evening. A good scratch required all four paws working vigorously through the side and belly hair, and even from 50 metres away you could hear those razor-sharp claws raking the dried skin.

One of the stranger biological links between badgers and humans is a shared species of flea, although perhaps a more inspiring sense of common ground arises from the abundance of historical marks that both of us leave in the landscape. Whenever I go badger watching I am always overwhelmed by the deep sense of tradition that surrounds their lives. It is not just the network of visible tracks, worn through years of passage up and down the hillsides, nor is it simply the tonnes of hard, red, clay-rich soil heaped outside the sett's complex of holes. It is also the small things.

Some of the details at this sett are the oily marks and pied hairs left on part of a lime-tree trunk where the badgers, each in turn, slump with ursine contentment to perform their elaborate groom and toilet. One can imagine the same routine not just tonight, but every night of every year, generation after generation. There is so much evidence of industry around a badger's dwelling one could easily feel it appropriate to invoke John Locke's principle that toil itself conferred a legal right to the land. Yet we should perhaps be wary of such dangerous notions: the badgers' title deeds will almost certainly long predate our own.

28 April 2003

Longnor, Staffordshire

When it appeared it looked like an inverted white triangle, which had rather incongruously materialised at the mouth of the hole. However, through the binoculars we could tell instantly that it was an animal's head and that it was bisected by those two black stripes to form the most distinctive pattern on any British mammal. It was a badger emerging from its sett.

It pushed its snout towards the evening sky and sampled the air and its accompanying atmosphere: a blend of rabbit scuts in the half-light, blackbirds chinking wildly from their roost in the lime trees above, a shovelful of blinking stars overhead and a cold night wind sweeping across the hillside.

Badgers may have a remarkable sense of smell and acute hearing but their vision is poor. None of the five animals that eventually emerged spotted us on the hillside opposite. There were seven of us, of three Cocker generations, lying in silence among a few hawthorns and completely mesmerised by the unfolding vision.

The most captivating moment came when a couple issued simultaneously from the same hole. After the customary nervous air-sampling routine they both got down to the evening's first task: a prolonged and clearly satisfying scratch. One of them slumped its solid bulk against the bank and got to work, even using its hind legs in a curious simultaneous action on the lower vent. It then perfomed the same comical two-handed operation on the upper belly. As it alternated between these operations, punctuated by the odd sideways chew at its flank, one conjured an image of the badger's subterranean life, particularly the musty flea-infested heap of vegetation that must serve as its bed chamber.

30 April 2012

BLACKWATER CARR, NORFOLK

In the bushes all around me as I write there are five or six willow warblers now singing. The sound they yield seems as fresh as the flush of yellow on the sallows in which they hide. Yet in any top ten of our summer visitors the song of the willow warbler probably wouldn't rank very high. The species produces an exactly repeated, gently descending cadence of what sounds (to my unmusical ears) like about a dozen notes. It has nothing of the force or show-stopping variety of a nightingale. Nor does it possess the eerie otherness of a grasshopper warbler's prolonged ventriloquial reel. Yet it is capable of having a large impact upon us and somehow it seems to soften the atmosphere of early spring.

My most memorable encounter with this effect occurred during my childhood. Willow warblers are Afro-Palaearctic migrants, wintering in a wide belt of sub-Saharan Africa then spreading to breed across the boreal regions of Eurasia, from easternmost Siberia to the Atlantic coasts of Ireland. In the 1970s I used to intercept this momentous inter-continental wave – at one time possibly involving as many as two billion birds – in northern Derbyshire. When willow warblers suddenly arrived there en masse the songs of the rival males constantly overlapped, so that their collective music fell on the grim, post-winter world of those gritstone hills like a warm shower of rain. Like rain, willow warbler song is soft enough to split rock and to soothe the human heart.

Strangely I seem to love it more when I cease to focus on its novelty and it becomes a subliminal pleasure. For then the sound is an audible analogue of that wider sense of luxury and nonchalance at the heart of summer. Alas there is now less scope for complacency than there used to be: willow warbler numbers have fallen like a stone in the last thirty years, declining possibly as a consequence of habitat loss and climate change by 60 per cent.

MAY

2 May 2011

Claxton

Aside from the odd globe of golden yellow thrown out by flowering marsh marigolds, Ducans Marsh is dominated by the copper colour of the dead rushes. It still seems a rather dormant landscape, but as I walk through the vegetation I realise that it is the scene of a life-and-death drama. Evidence of this quiet killing is brought to me intermittently when my coat becomes plastered with a rather unpleasant skein of old silk and the husk-like carcasses of dead St Mark's flies.

The agent of the carnage is called *Larinioides cornutus,* the furrow orb-web spider. I slowly realise that they are stationed right across this marsh in almost every spike of last year's marsh thistle and black knapweed. These hollow stems stand high above the general canopy of the rushes and catch the breeze with its cargo of innocent flies. In each of the locations the arachnid architecture is much the same: a female spider winches together two or more stems of the hollow stalks and then wraps around the point where they touch a protected couch of white silk. From this private retreat emanates the web itself. Look closer still and there she is – a glorious creature with two waving lines of chocolate converging at the rear of her mushroom-coloured abdomen.

Conventionally we think of spiders as rather niggardly predators. True to form, I touch my pen nib into the mouth of her silky bed and she immediately advances, all waving legs and open jaws. Yet this particular group of spiders is characterised by a massive rounded abdomen that looks disproportionate to the rest of the animal. As well as being beautifully patterned, furrow orb-web spiders have a wonderfully gravid, even feminine, shape. While each one of them might preside over a charnel house of black flies spinning gently in the breeze, we should recall that every dawn she gifts to us the sight of those dew-crusted webs glittering in the low-angled sunlight.

3 May 2010

CLAXTON

'Dawn chorus' is a funny name for that period when the birds start singing each day, because it does not really occur at dawn and it's certainly not a chorus. The exact time it begins here at present is 4.40 a.m., which is some way before true sunrise and is the moment when the night-time sky and the landscape first start to separate from one another as muted shades of grey. We should also think of it not so much as a united performance by the birds but more, perhaps, as their version of territorial warfare conducted through music. The architecture of the sound doesn't even suggest the idea of a collective endeavour. It is more that period when each member of an orchestra plays randomly for themselves while tuning their instruments.

I can hear various vocalists, such as wood pigeons with their hoarse soporific drone that seems so appropriate to this drowsy hour. Then there are the cockerel's clean-cut howitzer notes, which arc from across the fields smack into our garden. But blackbirds predominate and behind the mellow musings of the male, perched on our gutter, I can pick out, fainter and fainter, the recessional of others in Claxton. I think of all those blackbird males' crocus-coloured bills, which take their cue to open and sing from that exact instant of light's return. Given that this pre-dawn moment is not at precisely the same time in different parts of Britain, we cannot conclude that they all sing together as one. Yet we can envisage it, surely, since blackbird territories jigsaw across this country from Stornoway to Ramsgate, and from Wick in Caithness to Kenidjack in Cornwall, as high-curling waves of green music rolling outwards from 4.5 million voices. And since birdsong is the energy derived from sunlight and from landscape (soil, vegetation, insects, etc.) expressed simply as sound, perhaps you should think of those blackbirds as the self-delighting voice of Britain itself musing on the joys of spring.

4 May 2009

Claxton

A male marsh harrier lingered persistently over one area and was clearly intent on something below. The normal mode in a hunting harrier is a low-level manoeuvre angled against any breeze for lift and shaped by passages of deep, slow, languid beats interspersed with effortless glides, when the wings are upheld in a shallow V. This bird, however, ranged back and forth over one spot, turning with the breeze to go back to this same space. The flight, vigorous, erratic – a blend of swoops with long legs dangling, then wind-borne ascents and tricky breeze-ruffled jinks or turns – reminded me of a boxer looking for his opening. I eventually reached a position where I could see that he was actually loitering over a pair of mallard compressed tightly around their ducklings in a water-filled dyke. The harrier had them corralled but couldn't find a way past that mass of adult body and upraised beak. The female duck also launched powerful counter-attacks, propelling herself skywards, wings virtually closed, and then fluttering back down heavily.

Try as I might I couldn't avoid a flood of moral reflections seeping into this tableau and filling it with a new kind of story. Her courage, her persistent selfless defence, was the unavoidable centre of it. She shadowed those ducklings so closely I couldn't even count them. Her wild sorties at the raptor looked suicidal (the drake, by contrast, seemed far more unengaged by the fate of his own innocent offspring). Then it occurred to me: what of the harrier's persistence? What about his determination and duty in the succour of his own genes (perhaps lying enfolded within the eggs, still waiting to hatch)? Was he not also the good father, as she was so evidently the good mother? I thought finally, once this stalemate passed (as it did just ten minutes later), of how those yellow-downed ducklings, upending with comic intensity, would later snap up snails and whirligig beetles to pulp down in their tiny beaks.

8 May 2006

CLAXTON

It was a classic grasshopper warbler moment, which conveyed so much about this wonderful bird's character. Two of us heard one singing for the first time this year and we walked towards where we assumed it was perched. There came a second short song passage and without any hesitation both of us pointed to where we thought it was coming from – in completely opposite directions. What a ventriloquist!

It does it partly by rotating its head to spray the sound in all directions, but the other half of the trick lies in the character of the song itself. A single dry note repeated sometimes for minutes on end, it's a rolling purr that is totally un-birdlike. The sound is far-carrying yet it is also so soft that it will often fall silent and yet you think you can still hear it. Eventually you realise: you're listening to the rustle of the breeze through the grasses or simply the sound of your own imagination. Textbooks make comparisons with fishing reels and the bird's name gives you a clue. Yet it's far more strange than the song of any insect. I suspect it's the lack of what one might call auditory architecture that makes it so difficult to pin down. Sometimes it seems as if the earth itself were humming a gentle subterranean hymn on the arrival of spring.

Even after you have fixed his location you do not see the musician himself, who is buried deep within the vegetation. It may sound perverse but I love the fact that you hardly ever see grasshopper warblers. It reassures me that there is unspeakable mystery in this over-domesticated landscape of ours. Of all the thousands that have been caught and ringed in this country, just thirty-two have ever been retrapped. Among the millions that breed across Eurasia I suspect many will wriggle their subtle mouse-like ways between here and west Africa never once being glimpsed by humans in their entire lives.

14 May 2013

Claxton

It was not my first pike of the year. Earlier this month I found the monster in miniature, five inches long and inert aside from the restless to and fro of the anal fin, the creature's outline broken by the shade of surface weed when the tiger stripes were perfect camouflage.

However, this new one was the real thing. It was several pounds in weight and behind the gills its girth was so great it would have taken both my hands to measure the body's circumference. Yet the flesh at this point on the body was now scooped out and eaten. From my position on the opposite bank it looked as if the neck bones had also been severed. In fact, the whole pike's head, along with the signature smile of this guiltless killer, lay at an acute angle to the curving line of its body. And I imagined the fish's final moments: the otter, possibly only four times the weight of its victim, manoeuvring the huge prey out of the reeds and onto the bank. The pike would have been clamped by those long lutrine teeth and while the tail fin might have lashed and the gills pumped, it was of no avail.

How the otter never came to complete the meal I pieced together from the circumstances of my discovery. Just before I spotted the fish a man cycled past and must have disturbed the otter's feast, forcing the animal back into the water and downstream. I arrived at the scene of the kill just minutes later, with the pike's body scales already acquiring the pink-brown mottling of a fish carcass in sunlight. While I stood to puzzle on the tableau I caught the head of the otter returning. I instantly backed away and then a dark shape emerged from the grasses. I could sense the electric sensitivity of those wire-like vibrissae as they sampled the air. Alas the wind was blowing directly from me to otter and it never appeared again.

16 May 2011

Claxton

This year's warm spell has produced an extraordinary abundance of St Mark's flies, those black-bodied silent insects with drooping hind limbs and a crab-backed hump on their mid thorax. For most of us they dwell just on the periphery of our attention. In the same way that they gently fill the ether like upward-floating black petals, so they seem to pass out of this life almost as casually. In our parish they adorn every single spider's web that I have inspected. Otherwise the creatures spend most of their short lives drifting together around or above head height, concentrated on the lee edge of almost every bush and tree.

Yet when one troubles to notice St Mark's flies there is a mesmeric beauty to their collective movements. Follow the trajectory of a single insect among its kind, and you see that it inscribes slow-twisting loops and zigzags through the still air. There is a form of organised chaos to the shape of these clouds, because each fly spirals steadily through the leisured column of its neighbours, until eventually it reaches the outer edge of the group. At this point it then twists calmly to regain the inner sanctum of mid swarm. Then slowly it arrives back at the outer perimeter once more and repeats its inward-turning motion. By this elastic system, the swarm is always mutating, assuming a multitude of plastic, drifting, black-spotted shapes, but always retaining a sort of fluid cohesion.

The collective dance of these innocents creates a zany sense of surplus energy, which has been absent from the landscape until a few weeks ago and seems in many ways the very essence of spring. The visual impact of the creatures is also cumulative as they rise through the food chain. In the skies above Claxton they trigger the graceful slow-wheeling food flights of black-headed gulls, which turn sparkling, white then black, in a self-perpetuating envelope of their hard hungry *kraa* notes.

17 May 2010

Claxton

The St Mark's fly derives its name from the insect's supposed emergence on the allotted day of its eponymous saint, 25 April. Yet the flies are not as religiously observant as their name suggests. My first was on 19 April and they reached their greatest abundance by early May. They are hairy, black-bodied, long-legged danglers, with a swollen, slightly humped thorax and, in the males, rounded goggle-eyes. They have a lethargic manner that could easily be mistaken for menace. I have one resting on my cuff as I write these words; another moves furtively through my hair.

In truth they are really one of life's great victims. Their species' strategy seems to be to flood the market with their protein and then, with all their predators in a state of glut, to hope that at least some escape to breed. For now, every spider's web along my usual beat is filled with their dried-out black husk bodies, twisting and billowing on the breeze. In the silken den of a rather splendid orb-web spider called *Larinioides cornutus,* I notice how she has four stiff-bristled legs curved around the soft body of her latest immobilised fly.

Higher up the food chain, however, the same insects can also acquire an extraordinary precision of movement, because the gloriously deft summer falcon known as the hobby loves St Mark's flies. Overhead, the birds swing down to seize the prey as yet invisible to me. However, I am forewarned of the moment of impact because in the instant of connection the falcon seems almost to be struck by a pulse of electricity and the current momentarily disrupts the bird's own sweet flowing. The wings close forwards, the legs rise up and forwards and the insect is taken to meet the beak in one sleek action, and in the following split-second the falcon's normal flight blossoms once more from that awkward twisting motion of life into death, death into life.

18 May 2009

CLAXTON

There has been such a flailing horde of swifts over the marsh all week that one almost began to feel the shallow bowl of the Yare Valley had somehow magically corralled them here. But how do you confine a bird that seems to treat the whole troposphere as a playground?

Yet I did have one encounter that illuminated the species' key limitation – a black rag in the road that was still pulsing upwards to get airborne. It was a swift. One wing had been cheese-wired by the telephone cables and the main flight feathers were completely ripped off, while parts of the back were reduced to bare skin. I did the only (and most painful) thing I could. Yet you can see how it happens. There is a suicidal frenzy to some swift manoeuvres. In the chilly cloudier conditions of the last few days they have been at tree level and below, grazing hard down the cold air and then firing just above the ground so that, I swear, sometimes they touched the buttercups.

However, the week's ultimate swift moment came even earlier, when the whole landscape was flushed by a cold northerly airstream. It was so strong it blew away the swift scream, so that the tableau was played out in silence. At boot level the wind ripped down the river banks, parting and brushing the vegetation like someone blowing a cat's fur. In the sky above, successive fronts of rain cloud barrelled southwards and with each wave of blue-black the swifts rode ahead of it, presumably feeding on the insects compressed into the bands of warmer air. There was one intense moment – with the cloud wall pressing south and the green horizon of trees inked down to a blackish wash – when suddenly about seventy swifts speared together as a fizzing skein that unravelled almost as quickly as it had been wound tight. Higher still a hobby, the only predator with swift-catching capabilities, scythed by slowly.

19 May 2008

WHEATACRE, NORFOLK

The sudden flush of heat across East Anglia has set the farm fields racing skywards, and on the southern edge of the Waveney floodplain the world was divided into just two colours, the green spiring up and the blue pressing down. Yet one colour had also bled into its neighbour. The cow pastures at Wheatacre are made up largely of a flowering grass, rather oddly named 'Timothy', and there is a faintly bluish tone to each separate inflorescence of this species. When viewed in aggregate across the flats, the fields of Timothy made it seem as if that ozone blue had somehow come to Earth, secreting itself among the vegetation.

Over this shining green-blue landscape, which rippled gently in a cold westerly, butterflies struggled against the breeze. They were mainly whites but every now and then a peacock sallied across the grass canopy as a scrap of plush purple velvet. Above the butterflies, concentrated in linear plumes down the dykes, were St Mark's flies.

These bulbous-bodied black insects had drawn in a suite of predators, foremost of which were the hobbies. For that irresistible blend of economy with power, so much a signature of falcon flight, only a peregrine outdoes its smaller relative. The hobbies would swirl down in effortless parabolas and, at the moment of upturn, seize, kill, eat, and retrieve the sweet rhythmicality of their wing beat in one deft manoeuvre. Even the rooks seemed captivated, and in gauche movements they tried for the same fly-catching technique. Then one hobby spotted something larger, spiralled down and plucked it out of the air. It was so fast I couldn't follow the procedure exactly but, as the bird lifted again, four purple wings tumbled slant-wise with the breeze like petals freshly fallen from a tree.

21 May 2007

CLAXTON

Buttercups. Even the name hints at luxury. One wonders also if the associations with cattle and milk – since they were so often the dominant flowers in cow pasture – were deliberate. Or was it perhaps a classic example of the way that we've forged these links in our nomenclature completely unconsciously?

Whatever the truth, I cannot think of the buttercups of my childhood without imagining cows in the fields. Nor can I see myself then, except that I would be lying down among the flowers. They were everywhere, like scattered corn, and in this position we'd pluck one and perform always the same operation.

The gold corolla was poked beneath a brother's or sister's chin to see if they liked butter. I'm not sure why we did it. Whatever the weather or light, those glossy petals always gave the same answer. There would be the tiny yellow shadow on the under-chin to prove that butter was best.

The moment always had the same soundtrack. Over our heads were the cold trembling song of curlews and the emotionally far warmer, perhaps even slightly crazy, sky-dance of lapwings and the reassuring lifelong tick-tock of cuckoos. In fact, the plantation on the hilltop was known to us as Cuckoo Woods.

Now two parts of that Derbyshire chorus are gone, although the curlews are still singing. But to think that the buttercups have gone suggests to me the real craziness of this world. Recently around the Yare I saw some fields smothered in yellow, but they turned out on closer inspection to be always sow thistles or dandelions. There are a few buttercups in one small horse paddock, but not enough to rekindle that sense of childhood luxury. Railing at conventional poetics, Bertolt Brecht once wrote, 'To think of trees is treason.' Funny how things change. Not to think of trees – or the loss of buttercups – now seems a form of treason of its own.

23 May 2005

Claxton

One of my favourite garden visitors at this time of year is the orange-tip butterfly. Like many of our most charismatic insects it is now in decline. Its fortunes are pegged to the main foodplant – lady's smock – in turn a beautiful inhabitant of damp meadows, which is a component in our environment that is in short supply. Fortunately the butterfly is still common in the southern Broads, and in northern Britain it may be a beneficiary of global warming.

What is indubitably rare in British nature, however, is the touch of flame orange on each forewing of the male, from which it derives the prosaic name. (An older version, lady of the woods, seems far more expressive.) There are few instances of this same wonderful colour in our birdlife. The best examples are the kingfisher's breast or that lovely patch of sienna concealed under a lapwing's tail and only revealed in the bird's strange rump-in-the-air courtship wiggle. Despite its brilliance in the orange-tip, the colour actually has a protective function, since it tells birds how unpleasant the insect is to eat – a consequence of those bitter-flavoured mustard oils accumulating in the body as it munches on the foodplant.

Since the lady of the woods' upper wings are just black and white, she can easily look very plain. But certainly not when you study her with a ten-times hand-lens and so close that her compound eyes look like black-flecked green spheres. At this range the delicate marbling on the underwing expands into an entire landscape, with black and green rivers meandering across a great plain of white, dotted throughout with islands of yellow or green.

24 May 2004

CLAXTON

I have some inkling of what Henry Thoreau meant when he wrote, in his hymn to the power of dawn in the classic *Walden*, 'Morning brings back the heroic ages.' One senses that the landscape, rinsed down by the hours of darkness, is momentarily handed wholesale back to nature, while any dawn-awakened human is a mere spectator on this parallel new world. One memorable example involved a magnificent male pheasant strutting down the village street, bold as you like. It rose onto our fence, sauntered across the back lawn and out through the neighbour's garden.

Two other notable dawns include the day our daughter woke us to see the red-legged partridge perched on the roof of our car, a handy high perch from which to deliver its steam-locomotive's chuffing call. A hare cantering down our lane at 4.30 a.m. was a further salutary reminder that we are merely leaseholders on this patch of territory. More bizarre was a second hare sighting I had at about midday. This time a more hurried individual covered the same route in reverse, looking bewildered as if the noon sun had temporarily cooked his hare's brains.

Yet my most memorable experience of the intersection between the wild and the civil came just the other day. It was a female sparrowhawk heaped over a wood pigeon it had killed on the neighbour's drive. The yellow eyes were as blank as a shark's. Normally I resent the almost erotic fixation with predator–prey relations on wildlife television, but there was something mesmeric in the way her razor-sharp claws slowly, gently, kneaded the pigeon into extinction. Then off she flew, lugging twice her own weight with her. No lion on its buffalo kill could have been more compelling.

27 May 2013

Claxton

I love those archaic country names that define an animal by reference to another. A good example is the old Norfolk 'cuckoo's leader', which was used for that strange – alas now nationally extinct – migrant woodpecker, the wryneck. Better still are those titles that yoke together completely different organisms, such as 'cuckoo's shoe' for the bluebell. Best of all is the name in the local language: *botasen y gôg* is Welsh for 'cuckoo's boot', while *brog na chuthaig* is its Scottish Gaelic equivalent.

What these names do is pinpoint the experience in a particular soil, the names arising only where bluebells grow and cuckoos sing together. They are also rooted in time: those precise moments in the season when the cuckoo and the bluebell, so to speak, put on their shoes and dance as one. Finally we should recall that they arise in those souls who are profoundly alert to what sings at their feet or over their heads. So the name speaks of place, moment and of the human spirit that forged all the connections.

I want to propose a new name for the swift in our area: the 'water-lily bird'. Its origins lie in my daily spring walks along Carleton Beck in anticipation of both. The swift and the plant are in some ways diametric opposites: one ascending a few feet from the sub-aquatic sludge; the other surging pole-wards out of Africa. Yet they converge in the air of Claxton Marsh at almost exactly the same moment. That first swift – a bird that screams of the Earth's intricate interconnectedness – brings nothing less than a throat-tightening sense of reaffirmation, but then so too does the appearance of those great spheres of green, which seem heaven-sent symbols for the unity of all nature. In truth, I love those water lilies even before they reach the water's surface. Those weeks – when the crinkle-edged lettuce-green leaves, scrolled and vulva-like, wander slowly upwards through Carleton Beck – are filled with an immense sense of life's possibilities.

28 May 2012

BLACKWATER CARR, NORFOLK

For the first time this year the marsh is steeped in warmth and the pace of life is all at once more leisured, almost sluggish. The singular note of intensity on this otherwise lazy afternoon comes from a reed fringe in the dyke. It is the song of a reed warbler. It is a sound no mnemonic could convey – a medley of scratchy and guttural notes with a chugging engine-like rhythm, relieved occasionally by sweeter passages, and characterised overall by a mood of nervous repetition. In chorus, where the song of one bird overlaps its neighbours, the music of reed warblers becomes a never-ending river over the ears and it recedes into the background as a chaotic but somehow soothing flow. Together with the wilder and more assertive medley of its sibling, the sedge warbler, the reed warbler creates the summer soundtrack of the Norfolk Broads.

One intriguing element of sedge and reed warbler songs is their insatiable mimicry. Fragments of other bird vocalisations are learnt, perfected and inserted into their wild free-form performance. Suddenly out of the same wide beak comes a machine-gun rattle of blue tit notes, a dash of swallow, the sweet contact calls of reed buntings and a rendition of common whitethroat alarm sounds that are so note-perfect you would imagine the other bird is present. Research has shown that these borrowings enhance the attractiveness of their author and birds with bigger songs have more reproductive success. I also wonder whether the imitations serve as a kind of regional dialect that informs a female about her prospective mate. Does the full repertoire of his borrowings imply his familiarity with a very specific landscape that holds all the birds he copies? If he knows the neighbours, will he not know that particular neighbourhood intimately and be best adapted to navigate that place and all its resources? His song, in short, maps the locations where he is most likely to nest successfully.

30 May 2011

BERGH APTON, NORFOLK

This village-based sculpture trail is now such an eagerly anticipated fixture of the regional arts scene that it seems odd to have to recount the basic format. For three weekends (between 21 May and 5 June) vast numbers of the public can be found wandering the labyrinthine lanes that thread through this exceptional place. Mere strangers are then encouraged to let themselves into a selection of private gardens without so much as a 'Hello, dya mind?' to the owners, who are often on hand to facilitate your 'trespass'. These settings range from the vast parkland around Bergh Apton Manor right down to the maze-like arrangement of hedge, bush and outbuilding that encloses the village post office. In each of them is a display of sculptural work by a huge range of artists, many of whom have international reputations.

This year, as if sculpture were not enough, they have bolted on to the main show an array of music, drama, performance and rural craft displays, such as hedge laying and wrought-iron work. In some ways these 'extras' rival the central artistic event in terms of quality and value for money. However, I was reassured to find a good selection of work by some of my favourite local sculptors, such as the brilliant scrap-iron birds and beasts of Harriet Mead, the wonderfully mobile steel creatures of Andy Jarrett, the more decorative ceramics of Georgina Warne, and the calligraphy of Gary Breeze. And all that fresh air somehow liberates us from the usual wall-to-wall piety and deference that often cramp more formal art exhibitions. I loved the way the lady with the strong Norfolk accent and her Asda shopping bags felt entitled to argue how Chris Summerfield's *Fish on Wheels* (the emblem piece for the whole exhibition) should have really been sited over water. Somehow Bergh Apton allows us all to feel – well, for three weekends, at least – that sculpture is important but also part of our everyday experience, as beautiful and familiar as the trees and the sky.

31 May 2010

CLAXTON

They were not here now. Yet they had been. The area of Ducans Marsh where their play had been most concentrated was trampled flat into a flask-shaped patch of dead grass, five by two metres across its lower bulb, with a five-metre corridor – the flask 'neck' so to speak – running back into dense vegetation. From this latter cover there expanded outwards a separate network of trails across the marsh, and over every newly beaten path the rushes draped or folded downwards to convert each into a tunnel under the lush growth. One could easily imagine the fox cubs delighting in this labyrinth, bolting back and forth, chasing each other and exulting in their first tastes of shadow and spring sunshine.

Yet alongside these residual scenes of pure innocence were the killings and corpses that are indivisible from the presence of so many hungry canines. On the log bridge across the dyke was a pile of mallards' curled breast feathers, as if newly spilt from a torn pillow. Perhaps the most surprising of prey (can one possibly infer that the vixen had pandered to her youngsters' taste for sweetness?) were wizened sugarbeets gnawed to their tips.

Much more typical was the way their playground patch was strewn with pheasant wings, wood pigeons' tails, an indeterminate paper-thin breast bone and, most tantalising of all, the glorious vermiculated flank feathers of a drake gadwall. Fox turds and feather remains, different versions of the same prey, were promiscuously jumbled: gross and mysterious, innocent and macabre.

I finally followed the maze of trails until it led me back to the earth from which these exuberant yearlings had emerged blinking into sunlight. From the dark cavity among the tree roots I could look back across the whole scene of their last few weeks. I felt I could see it as those cubs had seen it: that rising surge of cow parsley, the sunlight on the open marsh and that whole wide new world beyond the shadows.

JUNE

1 June 2009

Claxton

The light and chlorophyll have done their work in the past two months to seal up Decoy Carr in a vast network of shadow and leaf. The oak and alder trees have broken bud and roofed the wood, while a vast choking scramble of nettles and cleavers has risen from below, so that any sense of the solid ground has more or less gone. The only open space left is in between – from the canopy down to about the height of a man's chest. Moving through the place feels at times like doing the breast-stroke in green water. Worse still, the lower vegetation is furred with bright toxins. (I have one nettle sting beneath my wedding ring that has persisted for days.) If I had to represent this magnificent spot as an abstraction it would be as a ragged-edged black block with an intense green sphere at its centre. It's a place where life is almost suffocating upon itself.

Noting the wildlife was a chancy business, because most of it was perched on the leaves of nettle, such as the tens of thousands of copse snails and common amber snails. When the hoverflies *Rhingia campestris* navigated the nettle forest, their orange abdomens seemed almost to glow, although not as brightly as the cardinal beetles, whose terracotta-red bodies have a lustrous sheen, while their shiny black legs look as if they are fashioned from black wire. Yet there was one brighter, unequivocal moment of pleasure and revelation on which my visit turned. A vixen shot away, but not without delivering a strange, very dog-like warning bark as she fled. I hid to see who that counsel was for, and down through a bank of nettles, as excited and astonished by this place as I, threaded a fox cub about the size of a half-grown kitten.

2 June 2008

CLAXTON

It was one of those spring days when the swifts were moving en masse through the Yare Valley. Usually the species is a good barometer for wider conditions. In high pressure systems they tend to fly high overhead, but in poor weather, when insects are feeding at low elevations, swifts follow suit. Today was strange: some birds were way up in the ether appearing as thrip-sized specks against a vast ocean of cloud, but others were so low they must have been flecked with droplets of last night's rain as they winnowed just over the horizon of grasses.

Their low-level circuit involved spearing down the length of Carleton Beck and along its banks, which were a continuous white slope of flowering cow parsley. These close-focus views allowed you really to appreciate the strangeness of swifts. At this range it was not a case of effortless grace; their movements were full of labour and oddly asymmetrical. Each wing seemed to function separately and the whole creature looked so weirdly proportioned it was as if you were seeing just a part of a bird – the tail or simply the wings – with the power of independent flight. They flailed down the contours of the vegetation and the whole landscape became swift-sculpted, the wings shearing out waste, reaving the valley of all excess.

I went back down to the marsh towards dusk and they had gone completely. The air was cold and had congealed to such an absolute stillness I could distinctly hear the feet of a foraging vixen thrum across the ground as she pelted for cover. A mist was starting to spread around the hocks of the black heifers and their hot musty breath fired down into those gathering pools as twin jets of smoke; while along the dykes the damp air muscled and swelled up then arched out on to the neighbouring fields like the white-smoke tendrils of a ghost bramble bush.

11 June 2012

Claxton

I paraphrase what he said but Isaac Newton, despite initiating a revolution in scientific understanding, once suggested that he'd done little more than stand on the edge of life's oceanic mysteries and pluck pebbles from the shallows. One can tap into that feeling every sunlit spring morning by standing to admire the bumblebees. I recommend it heartily. Wait by the flowers and watch them traffic back and forth. Follow one for a few seconds and you'll quickly appreciate the insatiable busyness of these wonderful creatures. We often think of them as amiably slow but the sheer speed with which they assess each flower, take nectar, or truffle through the pollen and move on to the next bloom is astonishing. In a minute they can cover hundreds of flowerheads. Because we're allowed such prolonged views of a cluster in aggregate we assume we have the chance to study them. Again I recommend you follow any single bee. Within a short while the foraging ceases and the bee will swing windward and rise high over the garden, vanishing into the horizon sometimes at canopy level. So much of bumblebee lives is spent in perpetual transit and even when you find a nest its happenings are subterranean and largely hidden.

Equally unsatisfactory is to stand near a flowerbed and watch the collective pattern of their purposeful flight-lines criss-crossing the heavens in all directions. One consolation is to imagine that it is air traffic entirely for flowers, centred on sweetness and motivated by brilliant colour. The interlocking whizz of their passage is nothing more than nectar and pollen converted to movement and sound. Then one is occasionally allowed something a little more intimate, such as the time recently that an early bumblebee landed on my leg and, angling its long pointed tongue down, proceeded to slurp up some vital salts. I like to think of my micro gift of savouriness on its own separate journey into the mysterious hidden world of a bumblebees' nest, carried in a bumblebee's stomach and there exchanged in the dark warmth of its nest, from sister to newborn sister.

13 June 2011

CLAXTON

It is the curse of every naturalist. People find injured creatures and assume you can help. I seldom can. I lack totally that blend of nurse-like practicality and Franciscan patience that is required to nurture the injured wild animal back to health. Yet this poor creature was a common swift so how could I refuse?

The injury scenario looked pretty familiar. The swift couldn't fly and immediately next to the spot where it was found was a starling squashed in the road. Swifts and starlings are mortal enemies and compete fiercely for nests in our roof space. Last year in our village I came across a starling attacking a grounded swift. Had I not intervened it would have severely injured or killed the bird. I rescued it in my hands and watched it spiral slowly upwards, only for the starling to fly at it again and wrestle the swift to the ground in the middle of the road. I then chased off the aggressor and let the bird go a second time. It flew away rather shakily and low over neighbours' gardens and even then the starling darted directly after it and was in hot pursuit when I lost sight.

There is an excellent website on helping grounded swifts. One revelation was that one shouldn't throw them into the air, as I'd always assumed, but let them take off from your palm. It also suggested that the chances of survival are best among freshly emerged, rather overweight juveniles. Our bird, alas, never flew again. Yet it gave me strange new sensations of the species. One was the simple feeling of pity. Swifts are such consummate beings – one usually stands in awe at their reckless brilliance, at their screaming high-wire act – one forgets that they occasionally fail. The other revelation (given that the scientific name, *Apus apus*, means 'footless') was the way the powerful little feet and sharp claws dug into my finger like a silent plea for help I could not give.

14 June 2010

Claxton

I know the name doesn't conjure a thing of particular beauty, but for my money hogweed is one of the glories of Claxton in June. In the past we may not have appreciated its strange, robust aesthetics, but we definitely valued the plant for its utility. The reference to pigs (like the alternatives of 'cow-cakes' in Somerset or 'cow clogweed' in Scotland) drew on the fact that it was gathered as fodder for livestock. According to Geoffrey Grigson's wonderful study of plant culture, *The Englishman's Flora*, its leaves and shoots taste of asparagus and he knew even in the 1950s of farmers who bundled it up for the sty.

It's not only a plant for summer. I love it just as much in winter, although its effects upon us are then largely subliminal. Those huge triffid-like columns that look so ineradicably healthy now, wither and dry slowly over the autumn until they are mere hollowed-out skeletons by November. When the snow falls the residual architecture of its multiple stems and umbels often catches the snow so that the hogweed buckles under the dead weight. But still the plant stands: defiant amid the grey skies and whitened landscape, hogweed seems to persist as a monument to a glorious sun-blessed planet we once inhabited and called 'summer'.

I have to confess I have a very particular relationship with the plant now because I have acquired a passion for photographing insects. My two girls, who themselves have grown like hogweed in recent years, beg me not to tell anyone, lest they think me strange. One of my curious activities is to stand by the hogweed to observe its millions of visitors. Other members of the umbellifer family draw in the beetles and the hoverflies, but nothing quite magnetises the invertebrate world like flowering hogweed. Insects seem to luxuriate in those vast fresh plates of whiteness and I and they attend the plant like so many worshippers at a shrine.

18 June 2007

CLAXTON

In the Yare Valley the only thing to break the absolute flatness of the marsh is the network of gates and upright posts that give access to every field. I've come to love these isolated architectural structures, which, in aggregate and when viewed from any distance, seem to link up across the flats like a gigantic artist's installation.

I walk out to inspect one old post. It stands about 1.5 metres tall and 30 centimetres wide and is a favourite perch for hunting barn owls. The wood is weathered to a fine grey-green and has a felted softness to my touch. I give up trying to age it after sixty growth rings and try to imagine it as a living tree, its long sentinel years, the thousands of birds and millions of invertebrates to which it gave life.

Along some of its growth lines the post has cracked during its half-century standing here and the crevices shelter a host of residents. A black ant makes a speculative foray up one side; down another dashes a spider, mottled beautifully like an owl. When I look closer I see the reason for its outing: a small fly has been lassoed by a line of silk from which it dangles helplessly. Through the lens I can see that the spider has sucked it completely dry and the chitinous fly remains to spin and billow gently in my breath.

In other crevices I find more spiders, weevils, beetles, and a red mite with tiny white hairs on its back. This single upright post occupies no more space on the marsh than the sky is filled by the hobby hawking dragonflies briefly over my head, yet it is a whole world unto itself. When I look back across the line of my approach to this 'world' I'm appalled by the clumsy trail I've cut through the grass. Like a logger's road through the tall surrounding forests, it is as clear as the marks I've just made on this paper.

20 June 2005

CLAXTON

I could see the dragonflies – four-spotted chasers – hurtling down the longitudinal strip of air above the weed-topped water's surface. Every so often one would stop before me as if to scrutinise the intruder, then it would make a sequence of straight-line movements in several planes, but so fast it was difficult simply to keep my eye trained on the zigzag passage. Just occasionally, all this glittering and predatory dynamism would come to a full stop, when it would land on a grass blade by the dyke edge. Unfortunately, I had only to make the gesture of a movement in its direction to trigger the electric-fizz flight once again.

Later, however, I found a four-spotted chaser fluttering in the vegetation. Initially I thought it was an adult newly emerged from the larval envelope called the exuvia, but I quickly realised that it was damaged. Part of an outer rear wing had not properly developed and it was unable to fly. Deformity in wild animals is rarely observed. Most that we see are, in the truest sense, living perfection. Occasionally one finds a bird with aberrant plumage or, more rarely, with a deformed beak or foot. Toeless street pigeons are probably the commonest example.

I lay down and encouraged the insect to clamber into my hand where I could scrutinise it more closely. In every other way it was flawless, right down to the remarkable copper-coloured compound eyes, whose sensory cells showed in all their dazzling symmetry through the hand-lens. Despite the insect's near perfection I realised as I stood to leave that its momentary and weightless impression on my palm was probably the sum of its legacy to the rest of life.

23 June 2003

CLAXTON

As I rounded the woodland edge I spotted the foxes relaxing in a newly mown hayfield. The vixen was simply enjoying the sunshine, but her two well-grown cubs lolloped over the parallel heaps of cut grass, or occasionally came together in bouts of mock-fighting. One would collapse on to its side and look up while the other would stand victorious, front legs akimbo, head shaking as if it were worrying an old carcass. Then the roles reversed and the conqueror would become conquered. Finally the scrap fizzled out and both returned to their mother, who simply looked up, blinking against the strong light. With typically maternal affection she licked one of their necks before he tired of the fuss and strode off to stalk pheasants.

A fortnight ago I had stumbled on this same family sunning itself on the edge of a plantation. The spot was strewn with the remains of pheasants, red-legged partridges and at least one unfortunate shelduck, which nest in the nearby haystacks. I doubted that the present stalk would result in the cub's next meal. Two cock pheasants watched it approach them and eventually they were just metres apart. One wonders what cognitive process allows the birds, which seldom seem particularly intelligent, to recognise that this particular fox presented minimal danger. The birds danced and shimmied a little at the cub's movements then, like him, strutted off, counting the whole affair a draw. Not so the vixen. She had picked me out against the woodland and her gaze never deviated. I slunk into the trees to try to allay her fears but when I re-emerged the field was bare and I was sad to have disturbed the family scene.

27 June 2011

SALTHOUSE HEATH, NORFOLK

The best story I know to indicate how difficult it is to find nightjars on their nests is one told by the ornithologist John Walpole-Bond. He recounted an occasion when he came upon a nightjar's tail feathers all arrayed in the exact spot where they'd been 'plucked' by the foot (or hoof) of some unwitting pedestrian. It says much about a nightjar's camouflage but also about the extraordinary tenacity of these birds. Our nightjar was a few metres away, but she betrayed no anxiety except to keep her pale lids fractionally open so that we could see a third of her liquid dark eyes.

At such range we could observe every detail in her plumage: the six creamy spots down her grey-marbled shoulders, the rosette of black-edged throat feathers and the strangely thin beak with its protruding nostrils and then those remarkable whiskers around the mouth sides that help guide her insect prey (beetles, moths, etc.) into that vast pink maw as she feeds on the wing.

Throughout our visit she never moved a fraction. She was, in a sense, what she seemed: a dead log embedded in dead bracken. Yet this bird was both profoundly alive and deeply moving. Our moments with her felt like an act of worship at an ancient shrine. There is a glorious passage by Henry Thoreau of his encounter with a nightjar relative called a common nighthawk. Despite writing on 7 June 1853, Thoreau divined through his exquisite sensitivity to living nature how long these birds have truly been on Earth. He talked of her being like a 'bronze sphinx' and 'a relic of the reign of Saturn'. Writing before any of us had worked out that life has been unfolding for 3.5 billion years, Thoreau sensed that his bird pre-dated humans and even their gods. Proto-nightjars have been discovered in deposits that are forty million years old. Somehow all of that nightjar inheritance was there before us in her all-seeing, stone-like quiescence.

JULY

3 July 2006

Claxton

The first sound I heard as I walked down the lane was the burbling song of a swallow while it flew overhead. And that's how dawn came to me, as a sequence of sounds and smells rather than in any visual form. On the marsh the scent of new-mown grass carried an unmistakable hint of very distant cigar smoke. In the still-starlit sky there was already a skylark, but the song that arrested my attention was that of a reed warbler. Several times it repeated a near-perfect imitation of a kingfisher. The original bird makes a high, clean piping sound and if one could visualise the call, it would look like a streak of silver, a long-drawn ripple, running down the middle of the water.

Then the dawn came in such varied form – the clyping notes of oystercatchers, a crow overhead, the squealing of moorhens, the 'plop' of a submerging water vole – that it was impossible to keep tabs on it all. But at 3.38 a.m. I caught the first hint of the bird I went to hear. I urge you to enjoy it one more time, because blackbirds will fall silent in about a week and you won't hear them again until next March. At Claxton they all seemed to start together so that the deep, rich, effortless song rose up from the woods all along the marsh edge. The line of oaks was still completely immersed in shadow, and they sat on the horizon as an undulating dark ribbon. I imagined those softly contoured mounds as the dark loam of the blackbird music itself, rising up fresh from the earth.

Dawns always have surprises. This time it was a fox, a neat dark vixen with a pronounced limp in her right forepaw. She never saw me. I was totally still and quiet. She too was silent, gagged by the slumped body of a moorhen tight in her jaws.

4 July 2005

Claxton

I find it intriguing how a passion for natural history reorganises one's sense of the seasons. To many it might feel like midsummer, but if you scrutinise the activities of birds and plants they're obviously working to a different timetable. Rooks and jackdaws have finished breeding, and when not feeding their clamorous offspring they are dropping their feathers one by one. Moult is a classic indicator of autumn. If that weren't bad enough, the birds have even resumed evening flights to the roost, which is a sign of winter.

If you won't let me declare the end of summer then I'll call this moment willow-seed time. The trees along the road have just shed countless floss-winged seeds, and I love to watch the corridor of blue overhead where the drift is thickest. Occasional gusts send spreading pulses of gossamer into the tracks of sky-trawling swifts and one wonders if the birds ever rise higher simply to escape the ceaseless up-drizzle of white.

My other pastime is to sit and watch it ghosting through the arch of shadow between our holly trees, where the light conditions best reveal the stream-like flow. It has a hypnotic slowness. In more fanciful moments it suggests the fallout from some strange, innocuous chemical warfare, as if the neighbouring parish wished to blanket us in willow forest. The floss has remarkable adhesive qualities, and it gathers along the otherwise invisible strands of spiders' webs, betraying the architecture of these insect traps. Unfortunately (for the more house-proud of my neighbours), the web-revealing effect is just as strong inside a property as it is outside and around the garden.

5 July 2004

CLAXTON

The recent mixed weather has given me two contrasting visions of one of my favourite birds, the common swift. The first occurred in the Yare Valley, at the point where it widens to a large plain called Haddiscoe Island, whose emptiness was suddenly mirrored overhead by a great sparkling ozone. The birds were so high they looked like nothing more than black arrows sweeping in and out of the clouds. Their movements were random and playful and there was something in the way they porpoised into that vast blueness that made them seem as utterly remote and unattainable as those weird underwater creatures with bug eyes and gaping mouths that live in total darkness on the ocean floor.

The following day, however, they were suddenly much more intimate and accessible. A mountain range of thundercloud had pushed them downwards almost to head height over the village. They careered towards the houses opposite where they nest – how I resent the fact that the birds prefer their roof space! – before breaking away. It looked like a failed attempt at entry to the nest chamber, but swifts are so consummate in their aerial manoeuvres that it's hard to believe anything they deliberately undertake can end in error.

Then, finally, they returned. The half-metre wings collapsed awkwardly, scraping the gutter edge as they concertinaed to nothing, and the bird itself vanished down its improbably small hole. The swift's conversion from black meteor to mere terrestrial animal also has an air of the miraculous, like a magical sword that can somehow be placed in a scabbard only a fraction the size of the blade.

11 July 2011

CLAXTON

In the psychology of naturalists there is always a blurred borderline between the idea of an animal being rare and it also being difficult to see. We tend to think of things that we encounter seldom as being somehow scarce. Yet it isn't always true. Common things can be just difficult to record.

The point was brought home to me last summer when I saw a purple hairstreak. It's a glorious but relatively small butterfly strongly associated with oaks. If you see them well they have a lovely and almost sparkling purple sheen, especially to the middle of the forewing. The problem with them is that they tend to live in the canopy of mature trees and therefore one has to watch intently for a creature that is just 3 centimetres in size, flying 20 metres over your head.

It seems extraordinary how I could have passed thirty years in the middle of purple hairstreak country having only seen a singleton. Last summer, however, I happened to find a second by accident just a few metres above my head. It allowed me to figure out both the correct search image and also the best technique for locating them. This summer I seem almost unable to stop seeing the butterflies. Virtually every large mature oak appears to hold them. The queen of our village, a 350-year-old veteran tree, is their favourite spot. Right now is the perfect time to look. The best part of the day is late afternoon or early evening, even as the sun is setting. I have found them sailing in little flighty clusters above and around the oak leaves. Then they will stop suddenly, perch on the exposed foliage with their wings closed above their heads. As they relax so they unfold, with head pointing downwards and wings held flat, but facing just fractionally north of the dying sun, so that they look like tiny ladies' fans glossed purple, lying in the green.

12 July 2010

CLAXTON

In high summer one of my favourite spots in the parish is a pair of massive railway sleepers that act as a bridge over Carleton Beck. It is a glorious place of deep clear water, of white and yellow water lilies and cool shade scooped by the willows from the sunlit grass and reed. Yet into this English river idyll is blended a whiff of industrial dereliction, via the tangy note of bitumen coated thickly over the cut ends of pine trunks that were laid crosswise years ago along the sleepers.

If I peer over the side I can see a thousand tiny holes drilled over the decades by some species of solitary wasp. Today, however, their yellow-banded occupants are not my goal. Nor is it the grass snake sidewinding smoothly through the beck. (Somehow one always watches that tiny head, and its yoke of yellow around the neck, all lifted marginally above the water's surface, and misses the whipcord of black-banded green that lashes behind.)

What I'm after is the most beautiful of all Claxton's dragonflies, an insect that is more lovely by far than its name, the banded demoiselle. As two males chase and fight, they go skittering over the water, each with four wings caught helicopter-wise in the brilliant sunlight as two interlocking hemispheres of brittle blue-green. Then when they land they become something neither Fabergé nor Cartier could have conjured even in their dreams: a scintillation of turquoise, those blackberry-black eyes bulging on stalks, those fantastical blue-gauzed wings and all of it the more precious for being so transient. It is the sort of creature that, come winter, I can hardly believe has ever existed.

14 July 2008

CLAXTON

Poised in the middle of the water, the mother mallard gave away his presence, and I instantly understood her panic when a brief eel-line of darkness broke the surface. Like her, I thought the otter was trying to seize her one surviving duckling, and I realised as she thrashed down the dyke that she was attempting to lure him away.

The otter surfaced twice, its broad head sitting squat upon the waterline, and then all went quiet. I followed gingerly along the dyke edge and within seconds there it was: a dark shape feeding lengthwise on the bank. At just five metres away I could hear every crunch of bone and the soft chafing sound of those long white teeth working the flesh. There was an open-mouthed relish to the way he gulped down his evening meal, but it was not duckling, as I'd anticipated; it was fresh pike. In the time it took to reach the spot, he'd caught the fish and eaten most of the body. He toyed briefly with a final morsel, but fish heads were not to his magisterial taste and, casting me a quick glance as he slipped back into the water, he continued fishing in an unhurried departure.

I never saw more than the head again. But the effect of his passage was as if electricity had been run down the length of the dyke and a shock administered to the whole stretch. The stems of reedmace shuddered with his subaquatic probings and the zigzagging lines of bubbles seemed to solidify on their journey upwards, breaking the surface like fragments of ice.

When the water resumed its customary stillness I went round to inspect the pike and the glass-splinter teeth inside its empty head. I didn't so much walk home. I seemed to float across the marsh by moonlight, and when I finally went to hang up my coat there was just the faintest trace of fishiness on my fingertips.

16 July 2007

CLAXTON

This month I made my maiden voyage into the pleasures of the moth trap. Basically, it involves a wooden box crowned by a bright light. The insects are attracted to the protected bulb and then find their way through a slit in the box's Perspex lid, where they settle for the night among a heap of egg boxes.

In the morning it's not so much a question of waking them up as admiring them in their new bed before tapping them out into the undergrowth, where they rest until nightfall. The pleasures are multiple and sharpened by my neophyte status, but one is the sheer challenge of identification. For instance the noctuid family numbers four hundred species and all are roughly a similar size but distinguished by subtle differences in an enormously complex sequence of patterns.

My all-time highlight was undoubtedly the moment I saw an eyed hawkmoth fluttering through the night grass towards the trap – a blur of greys and brown and unbelievable pink. Until the moment I spotted its plate in the book I didn't even know that this glorious species existed. Yet the thing I love most about the moth trap is that, in essence, it's an entire landscape distilled to these small exquisitely patterned envelopes of protein, which were earlier cut, larval mouthful by mouthful, from the leaves of sallow, poplar, hazel, birch and various grasses. Then through the alchemy of the pupal stage, the fully adult moths emerge. Paradoxically they invoke a landscape that is all around us but most of us have never seen. In the moth trap in the morning we are privileged to encounter this mysterious night place in an array of forms as strange and beautiful as anything conjured by hallucinogens. I am already completely hooked. It's merely a question of where I'll set the trap tonight.

23 July 2012

BLACKWATER CARR, NORFOLK

My acquisition of a tiny wood on the banks of the River Yare has allowed me to renew a transaction with nature that I haven't enjoyed for forty years. Every time I visit I permit myself the guilt-free pleasure of a thick fistful of plants in flower as a bouquet for the house. Alas, we live in such an age of hands-off environmental anxiety and in a landscape of such intense environmental impoverishment that the practice of gathering wild flowers is now a lost paradise for most of us. PlantLife, the environmental charity devoted to our national flora, suggests that we now have more flower-rich roadside verges than we do wild-flower meadows. Sadly the organisation counts its membership in thousands, while the Royal Horticultural Society numbers its own in hundreds of thousands. It says so much about our national culture: that plants sown, tended and owned by us are somehow so much more engaging than native blooms that spring up spontaneously without our leave.

At this point of the season my wood is steeped in wild herbage and to clear a path of fifty metres through the rainforest of towering green takes hours of scything. In places the great hairy willowherb, in which the site is particularly rich, is way over my head. Yet it is the meadowsweet that is most wonderful. When first emerged the nascent flowers are pendulous drupes of tiny green 'berries'. These steadily turn to a wedding-gown cream and finally they burst, each flower spreading with a dozen or so threads of yellow-ended sepals. In aggregate the millions of flowers form a cream haze across the horizon. No wonder it was once known as 'Queen of the Meadow'. Some suggest that meadowsweet has a sickly smell, but Gerard in his herbal said 'it maketh the heart merrie', and 'delighteth the senses'. People once covered the bed chamber with meadowsweet as a kind of disposable carpet, and to induce dreams scented of marzipan and honey.

28 July 2008

Claxton

The marshes are shimmering tonight. Who knows what they are – chironomid midges or gnats or some other imponderable fly species – but in the low-level light of evening, as I look towards the west, the black chitin of these noiseless millions catches the sunlight and it settles on my eye as a blizzard of sparkling dust motes. There seems a glorious tension, too, between the severely mown regularity of the grass surface and then this randomly dancing upper layer of insect luxuriance.

These swarms are one of the great gifts of high summer and, although I say they are silent, in a sense, you can also hear them. But I wasn't thinking so much of the low choral hum that the insects produce themselves. Rather it is the aqueous burble that the swallows make, and the raw screams of the hunting swift pack that churns the air layer just above the insects.

These wonderful summer sounds are also a product of the surplus insect protein, converted through the birds' digestive system into the music of swift and swallow. If one pares down the ecology of the sound one level further, one realises that it is the underlying vegetation, eaten firstly by insects, then by the birds, which gives life to the whole natural orchestra. Could one not say then, that, just as it shimmers, so the marsh sings to me this evening?

Earlier in the day I was gifted another form of insect music. The route to the marsh passes through a brief shady tunnel framed by oak and brambles on either side. Here the hoverflies love to feed on ragwort and the final blackberry flowers. These beautiful nectar-drinking creatures are truly lambs in wolves' clothing, since their striking yellow-and-dark stripes mimic the colours of the more predatory and dangerous wasps. As you descend into this small dell of summer light and shadow you feel your whole self enveloped in the softest drone like a warm pool after long labour.

30 July 2007

Ring of Brodgar, Orkney

It comprises just twenty-one free-standing stones, yet it vies with the 5,000-year-old Neolithic village at Skara Brae or even Kirkwall's St Magnus Cathedral as the most celebrated structure in this archipelago. The Ring of Brodgar was erected some time between 2500 BC and 2000 BC and originally comprised a perfect circle of sixty tall monoliths with an encircling bank and ditch that was 130 metres in diameter.

From the hill above I watched while the 150 occupants of four huge coaches debouched and then circumnavigated the monument. As I did so I began to wonder about the impulse that drives this fascination. Are the Ring's shape and building materials still tapping into some undiminished ancestral urge within us? Or is it the more limited and recognisable stuff of sightseeing: we're motivated to come and see what others have previously come and seen.

While walking the stones myself I wondered also how long people have been coming to this spot simply as tourists. The elements have dealt severely with most of the graffiti, the rain polishing the words slowly over the decades until they become the vaguest runes, but one illegible inscription I found was clearly dated 1826. Another, the most impressive, carved precisely in tall capitals, was the work of J ISBISTER in 1881. The graffiti has now become a part of Brodgar's receding commentary upon human fragility in the face of time's relentless passage. We know for sure, for instance, that all who carved these memorials and those who stood with them as the penknife scraped the stone, and even all of their children, have now passed on. Yet their age is nothing when compared with those who built this ring. And they too are as nothing when compared with the age of the stones themselves.

For all this, somehow, the stones also feel deeply a part of the moment: the surging belts of purple heather or the sunflower-yellow sheets of common cat's-ear and the languid shadow stains from the passing clouds.

31 July 2006

Claxton

It's been a standard experience recently to go down for breakfast and, on opening a jar of honey or jam, to find that black ants have been there already. Scanning the dining room I usually find a safari chain of their sisters, their stomachs loaded with ant-bite-sized quantities of our food.

Last night we had a more dramatic encounter because the muggy conditions triggered their nuptial flight. Suddenly every crack or joint in the pavements by the house seemed to yield its trickle of ants. Many were the same food-raiding workers we get indoors, but among them was a good proportion of the winged males. Most impressive were the virgin queens, who had probably seen the light of day for the first time in their pampered lives. They looked about ten times bigger than their labouring sisters and had long glistening wings. Occasionally I caught one of these royal females embarking on her wedding flight, when she hopes to be pursued by as many males as possible. The airborne sex is followed by her loss of wings and, if she's really lucky, the founding of her own new subterranean colony.

Unfortunately the ants' nuptial flights excite the attentions of far more than the odd enquiring primate. Swallows, swifts and starlings were massed above Claxton to gorge themselves on this momentary bounty. The queens are great bulb-bodied creatures with a lovely bronzy sheen on their fat gasters. Even I was tempted to give one a try, for in Africa the similar flights of termites were once a welcome source of fresh protein. However, the idea I cherish most is that the food chain that began in our kitchen cupboard may end in the wing muscles of those swooping blue birds and, through the agency of the ants, our peanut butter and apple jam, could become a swallow's joyous flight over the lush forests of Nigeria.

AUGUST

6 August 2012

Claxton

The swifts are going now from our village. In fact, the mad summer fire of their lives is going out not just here, but all over Europe. Perhaps we should pause to enjoy them one last time before the final few depart. I got an inkling that they were on the brink here when the birds all suddenly ceased their usual rooftop village chase and climbed way up until they were no bigger than insects. A single bolus of twenty to thirty swifts spiralled across the blue, hurling down their communal scream, swerving and twisting and suddenly splintering apart; then they would all come together and resume their crazy sky waltz.

I think the miracle of swifts, perhaps the miracle of all life, is made more apparent if you try to think of them not as birds, but as insects. For swifts are made from nothing but tiny invertebrates floating in the ether. A flock of thirty and everything about them – that noise, those scintillating movements, their feathers, those air-filled bones as light as grass – is a distillation of billions of insects. And when I say billions I mean it. A single mouthful of food passed from an adult swift to its chick can contain three hundred insects.

Alas, the miracle of swifts is fading. In the last decade they've declined in Britain by 40 per cent. You wonder if we all think swifts so miraculous that they'll trigger that final

Eureka moment when we really get it: that this whole living landscape is in our hands. Or will they join the turtle dove and skylark and hares and starlings and lapwings and bumblebees and butterflies and moths on that ever-growing list of loss, and will we continue in our unending, self-referential cycle to the drowning cry of 'double-dip recession', 'quantitative easing', 'economic growth'? Just as we might see the swifts' sky trawl as composed of nothing but insects, we should recall that our own little dance consumes every other living thing around us.

8 August 2011

M6, BIRMINGHAM

We were log-jammed for several miles on the eastbound lane. Yet it was striking how soon after we'd halted that a spontaneous air of holiday broke out along the carriageway. People were on their mobiles getting updates. They climbed out of their cars to stretch or smoke. From one vehicle came a snatch of *Test Match Special.* A Mr Whippy driver climbed out but realised he was missing a trick and soon we were all queuing for ice creams.

You could actually feel the air clear of fumes but I suspect it would only have been from some spot about 150 metres above the motorway that you could have appreciated fully how this great vale of brutal noise was so quickly turned into silence. Out of the unaccustomed quiet the cry of a buzzard – the high, long-drawn, faintly melancholic note – drifted.

There were some grasses and common orache in the central reservation and most striking were the spikes of fat-hen standing proud of the barrier. They had all the usual architecture and leaf shape of fat-hen but the whole was shrink-wrapped in a black skin of exhaust residue.

Then I noticed them on a plastic fragment from a lost wheel flap: field grasshoppers exactly like those in my garden. One hopped down and led my eye to the others. There was a whole colony trapped here in this no man's land of violent car roar and speed. These particular insects may never have been heard or seen by anyone for decades. And there it was unmistakably – the quintessence of an English summer – the terse melody of their love song, a low-pitched stridulation of less than a second repeated in series of two. Occasionally if rival males embark on a kind of musical duel they will chirp alternately, and sound like some busy gnome working a tiny pair of bellows. Just for a few minutes these lost insects were reunited with their wider world and enjoyed a little passage of ordinariness in their extraordinary lives.

9 August 2010

Rockland St Mary, Norfolk

There were seven species of grasshopper, almost half the Norfolk total, and they were all singing from one single patch of grassland – a melange of hissing and purring sounds of different pitches and varying lengths that was made all the more maze-like by the individual insects' huge ventriloquial powers. I'd hear one and presume it was just in front me, only for it to fade and recede seconds later as if it were way off in the distance. When I lay on our bed that evening I swear I could still hear grasshoppers of indeterminate species singing from out of the walls.

For all the confusion they might inspire I love the stridulations of orthoptera (their technical name, which means 'rigid winged'). Although each species produces identifiably different notes, they all have a quality of release, as if some pent-up force or energy were being slowly allowed to dissipate, like an outdoor tap left running but only just. The songs of grasshoppers seem at once both the consummation of summer yet also its simultaneous and mysterious dissolution. For this reason these small dry purring notes acquire a kind of poignancy.

One sound, however, has a capacity to inspire something more lively. The grasshopper discovery of my summer has been the widespread local presence of Roesel's bush cricket, a species that until recently was listed no further north in East Anglia than Essex. Like several other orthoptera, including the wonderfully named long-winged conehead, the bush cricket is on a northward march, possibly as a consequence of climate change. The first Norfolk record was in 1997. Now it seems to be everywhere. Its presence here is both a revelation and a joy, since the song, a long soft drawn-out reeling buzz, is one of the most resonant of all orthopteran melodies. Whenever I hear one I dig into the grasses at the roadside to reveal a weird armour-plated leggy brute who is as hideous as he is beautiful.

10 August 2009

CLAXTON

The morning chorus on Ducans Marsh is reduced now to two bird species, but they summarise the moment perfectly. There are the even, hoarse, crooning notes of wood pigeons, but intermittently through this drowsy sound comes a machine-gun salvo of wrens banging out from the wood to remind us that the season is not quite done. When both pass I finally hear the sound I came to enjoy.

To call it 'song' is stretching the point, perhaps, but it is a love note. You can create the sound of a dark bush cricket by pushing your tongue tip against the roof of your mouth and blowing ever so briefly and softly, so that it momentarily vibrates. Even this truncated purr somewhat overstates its character. It is so small and shrivelled that it barely warrants the name of sound and its main purpose seems to be to bring one's attention to dwell on the enveloping silence that is emphasised by contrast.

It seems almost perverse to suggest that one loves a sound so rudimentary, and yet I do. I love it most because it hints at the strangeness of the creature making it. Occasionally when a dark bush cricket gets going it fizzes briefly in a way that hints at excitement but also seems inadvertent; as if the purring had momentarily spilled out of control. Simultaneously it suggests the most minute passion, but also embarrassment.

Then you peer into the vegetation and catch this very English creature at its work. The insect is burnt-brown and bulbous, but at its forehead wave two thread-like antennae that are twice the length of the creature. From its mid-section rise those monstrous hind legs that are hinged high overhead – each half, femur and tibia, greater in length than the insect itself. They now propel the beast, covered in shame at its discovery, deeper into the shadowed silences of early autumn.

15 August 2006

Peloponnese, Greece

Bug-eyed and with a squat, half-egg-sized abdomen sculpted rather like a rattlesnake's tail, the cicada is an insect that looks straight out of some Gothic horror. Its long wings have tea-coloured veins and they spread over the body as a diaphanous tent, yet when they finally open the insect's flight is so clumsy that you cannot help but chuckle. It whizzes through the air like some tiny spacecraft on a mission, and if disturbed from its arboreal perch it crashes noisily through the foliage before droning drunkenly away. Several times the escaping bugs struck me by accident, one catching me smack on the forehead.

Who could believe such a shambling brute could produce such a divine song; a song to die for, or, perhaps, to die to? The male's organ of sound, lying at the base of the abdomen, is an area of cuticle known as a tymbal that can vibrate at 4,500 cycles a second. The noise it yields – a deep, insistent, throbbing buzz – is before everything a song of the sun. It lasts thirteen hours, from eight in the morning until the moment of nightfall. Just after dawn as the hard white Greek sunlight fires down, each cicada tunes up, linking its song to its neighbour's like synapses snapping together in a waking brain, until the whole earth is alive with sound. By mid-morning everywhere is submerged beneath the brutal drone. One finds it hard to imagine that it is produced only by insects. It is as if the baked Greek soil or its eternal cloak of kiln-fired olive trees were humming to the sun. By midday it has acquired a menacing claustrophobic power. Could one possibly drown in sound?

Cicadas have produced the ancient atmosphere in which all of Greek history has unfolded. Aristotle studied them. They sang while Pericles spoke and when the last Spartan fell at Thermopylae there was still the eternal Greek hum. Ulysses might have outwitted the Cyclops or quelled the silky allure of the Sirens, but when he finally reached Ithaca, he could do no more than sit and endure them. Not even Zeus and his family had a magic equal to these insects. As they went about their meddling in the affairs of men, these mere deities left nothing but god-sized cavities in the song of the cicada.

16 August 2005

CLAXTON

Although the meadow brown butterfly has declined severely from the time when there was hardly a field of grass anywhere in the country without its resident colony, it is still our commonest species. And while it might be the dullest of our butterflies it is inconceivable to imagine the British summer without it.

At Ducans Marsh dozens of them wander over the canopy of now exhausted grasses, occasionally fluttering up to drink the nectar of marsh thistles, before resuming their desultory course. The mid-brown of the upper wings blends perfectly with the sun-dried vegetation and the one small detail occasionally catching the eye is a triangular patch of warmer orange on airborne females. Yet as a meadow brown lands, when it usually collapses sideways to reveal just the underside hindwing, it assumes the colour of recently dried earth.

Some meadow browns seem an almost exact analogue for the spent condition of the season. During the course of their two-week adult life the wings become bleached to a dull sepia and the edges clipped almost as if a child has patterned them with a butterfly-sized pair of scissors. Occasionally they are so tatty it is a wonder they can fly at all. These 'bites' out of the wing edge can be the work of birds and are evidence – believe it or not – of a canny defence mechanism. At the moment the bird attacks, it is drawn by a sequence of dark spots on the meadow brown's underside and it is tricked into pecking at these rather than some vital organ in the abdomen. Thus the butterfly escapes with no greater loss than a little wing power.

20 August 2012

Cosford Hall, Suffolk

What is it precisely about spiders that makes them so disliked as predators? Why did the late, great Tony Hare, co-founder of the environmental group, PlantLife, always call them – a little tongue in cheek, it has to be said – 'the agents of Satan'? As Ted Hughes pointed out in his wonderful poem 'Thrushes', even our favourite songbird is a terrifying killer: 'Nothing but bounce and stab/And a ravening second.' In fact, the victim in the horror scene we witnessed is itself a predator. It was a dark bush cricket, that bumbling long-legged relative of the grasshoppers, whose soft chirrup is now the soundtrack to East Anglia's late-summer evenings. Perhaps we forgive thrushes and bush crickets because they serenade us with their songs; the spider, by contrast, is such a silent killer.

This one ceased sucking the last juice of a fly it had previously snared and dropped like fate to the bush cricket that had somehow tumbled into the web. The way the spider bound the victim was terrifying for both its speed and its efficiency. The spinner glands at the rear of her abdomen fired out a belt of silk strands as fine as mist. Yet in seconds it held the victim like steel mesh and all we could see of the bush cricket was the lemon stripe of its underbelly. Before the spider finally started to eat it, injecting her salival juices that dissolve the inner tissues, the bush cricket had hung briefly upside down from one long leg like a butcher's carcass dangling on a meat hook. I found it so macabre (since I love bush crickets) I suggested we free it, but the killer was actually a remarkable and beautiful beast. It was a wasp spider and this individual was one of only about twenty records ever in Suffolk (in Norfolk there have been just four). However, wasp spiders, first recorded in Britain in 1921, are spreading rapidly northwards, possibly aided by their predation of grasshoppers.

23 August 2010

CLAXTON

I'm glad to see that in our parish it's now official. Moths are magical. As confirmation we have a poster for our forthcoming village fete, on which one of the events is entitled Mark Cocker's Moth Magic. I entirely disown any personal contribution but I would never deny the extraordinariness of the insects themselves.

What I find harder to comprehend is how some friends, very often lifetime naturalists to boot, seem almost completely resistant to their charm. Yet one group of moths that usually galvanises attention, rather in the way that orchids seem to engage non-botanists, is the hawkmoths. Star turn in this wider ambassadorial role is the hummingbird hawkmoth, a diurnal species and a migrant that is more like an honorary butterfly or, for some, even a type of invertebrate bird, than a moth. Wildlife organisations routinely receive calls from people who see one and believe they have just encountered an actual hummingbird.

The individual that recently graced our buddleia patrolled the great cones of purple with that strange zigzagging erratic flight. Here, then there, then, instantly, gone altogether. If I managed to get really close I could hear the faint thrum of those fizzing wings, which, on photographs, showed as merely a blur with a hazy lozenge of pale peach visible in the hindwing. The extraordinary curving proboscis, the length of the entire insect, pierced down into the flower nectaries and gave a weirdly elephantine hint to the beast.

If that sounds exaggerated then the hair on the bulbous abdomens of hawkmoths truly make them seem mammalian, almost like tiny flying mice. However, this fur is remarkably delicate, rubbing off as the moth ages and as it comes into contact with foliage or flowers. The hummingbird 'hawk' in our garden bore upon its back (actually the thorax) telltale signs of senescence, the hair having worn through to a brown chrysalis-like epidermis below, a strange signifier of both its origins and its impending end.

25 August 2008

Rockland St Mary, Norfolk

I was intrigued recently to see a painting in the National Gallery by the Flemish artist David Teniers the Younger in which a rich man is being led to hell through a subterranean crypt thronged with bats and snakes. Is the bat's nocturnal lifestyle enough to explain these centuries of misrepresentation? Yet while there is definitely nothing evil about bats there is something decidedly liminal. Their wings are no more than a diaphanous parchment, the thickness of a grape skin, stretched over a spider's web of finger-bone. It produces a motion so twisting and elusive you sometimes wonder, as you try to follow one in flight, whether you're seeing the actual creature or just some fading mental impression of a flying bat superimposed upon the airy space where one has just been.

Their echo-location system is one of those truths that outdoes fiction. Bats blast their surroundings with a machine-gun fire of high-frequency pulses then wait for the rebounded calls, which are unscrambled in the bat brain as information on the relative distances and contours of an environment. Essentially they're hearing the appearance of a place. The system is so sensitive they can detect and avoid a wire the thickness of a human hair. They can identify an insect – and judge its edibility – by the way their echoes curve around it. One is flabbergasted not just by the idea of a world sculpted by voice, but by the inner labyrinth of the bat's neurological system, which allows the creature a flight of such intricate convolutions when effectively blind.

We followed our bat, probably a Daubenton's, on a bat detector, a device that converts the calls to sounds within the human range of audible frequencies. It was a thin metallic crepitation that intensified as the creature swirled down across Rockland Broad. At its closest, the bat's sounds acquired a tachycardia-like intensity and every now and then we caught the creature itself as a brief muster of skittering darkness.

26 August 2007

CLAXTON

On the face of it, the poplar hawkmoth might seem an uninspiring little creature. Aside from a tiny (and usually invisible) triangle of fox red on the underwing, it is almost entirely different shades of grey. Yet this one insect has added a whole new dimension to my natural history.

The first I ever saw was lying on the path as I went for the post. Inspecting this perfectly intact but dead insect was like finding a dinosaur's egg or a chip from a meteorite – inescapable proof of another time and place. What made the discovery all the more exceptional was that it was obviously a local resident. It was this paradoxical blend of the neighbour and the completely other that I found captivating.

The little beauty eventually inspired my buying a moth trap and, while this summer's trapping campaign is coming to a close, the poplar hawk has been with me throughout. Often they cling to the outside of the trap in the morning and easily transfer to your fingers, then to some convenient twig. What is most wonderful is the way they remain there unmoving until nightfall. Often I go outside to visit them at their temporary perch, just to lift my spirits as I work or to remind myself that such a fantastic creature really exists.

It may be grey but poplar hawks have a beautiful curving sinuous shape, with a downward arch in mid 'back' and upward turn to the pointed 'tail'. Overall it has the fluid tumescent-headed lines of a tadpole or, at the other end of the size spectrum, a sperm whale. A secondary sweeping line is performed by the antennae that curve back and around the bulb-like head. The tiny serrations along their length give to these feelers the character of prize horns from a wild sheep. Go in close with a magnifying lens and you encounter another world – a compound of the monstrous and of perfection.

28 August 2006

NORWICH

Sometimes naturalists have to wait many years for fulfilment. My friend is a classic example. As a child he roamed the fields of Sussex chasing butterflies with his nets and his dreams of catching the blue riband of British lepidopterists, the Camberwell beauty. This gorgeous creature, one of Europe's largest butterflies, has an upper wing of deep, rich, almost velvety purple-brown with a half circle of azure-coloured ocelli along its submargin and then a broad outer perimeter around all four wings of black-dusted cream yellow.

It has been recorded in Britain about 1,500 times, the first occasion in 1748 when two were seen floating around willow trees along Cold Arbour Lane in Camberwell. The record occurred at a time when the 'village' was a favoured haunt of lepidopterists and before (as one of their number so indelicately put it) 'the place was engulfed by the catastrophic growth of London'.

Camberwell beauty is a wonderfully apt (if a touch parochial) name for such a striking animal, but I also cherish an early synonym, the 'grand surprise'. Neither of the English names has quite the same meaning in Europe, where the species is relatively common. I've seen it on many occasions around the Mediterranean, but usually just overwintered individuals, without the pristine, almost shining quality of newly hatched adults. These emerge about July, sometimes in such large numbers that it triggers migrations to the north and west.

These wanderings explain the occurrence of Camberwell beauties in Britain, with the highest numbers arriving in 1846, 1872, 1947, 1976 and 1995. In fact, it was the penultimate invasion when I came close to adding the species to my own list. Alas I missed it, and have had to wait thirty years to put things right. Yet imagine the joy unconfined reserved for my friend. He had hoped to see one since childhood; just the other day – fifty years later – one happened to appear on the buddleia in his garden.

SEPTEMBER

3 September 2012

CLAXTON

We were breakfasting in the garden when there was a momentary flurry that broke the breezy atmosphere of swaying buddleia with its lazy scatter of butterflies. It was a synapse of intense connection between a peacock butterfly and a bird. In an instant, and even without my spectacles when the world is otherwise rather blurry, I knew it was a spotted flycatcher.

Nothing in Britain moves like a spotted flycatcher. They are strange, wonderful creatures of muted grey-brown and duller than any dunnock. Most of the time they sit on a wire or exposed perch, but completely still like a tiny wooden effigy or some long-winged sculpture. Suddenly the little icon breaks its stillness. It bursts into flight, describing long curves, even pausing mid-air, back-beating wings like a kingfisher's before a dive, when the beak snaps shut on its flying prey. Then back it goes. The wings close. The statue returns to its niche.

It is this alternation between quietude and drama that supplies a spotted flycatcher with all the chromatic riches a bird could ever need. It's a rainbow of colour expressed in movement. There is no hue quite like the species' mouse brown.

It was once present in churchyards up and down this country, where the flycatcher utilises the headstones as multiple perches. (In fact, the bird's greatest gift to us was probably this living intensity even among the places of our dead.) I use the past tense because the spotted flycatcher is part of the old–new story – 88 per cent of the British population lost in forty years.

Such long-distance migrants now inhabit a world of multiple jeopardy: climate change, habitat losses, desertification, pesticides. The whole machinery of this planet is jamming tighter and tighter around citizens such as the spotted flycatcher. If it goes completely, no human life will end, no human enterprise fail, and many will not even notice, but when this little pagan deity is gone one irreplaceable shade of colour will pass from the Earth's register.

4 September 2009

CLAXTON

This year it has been fascinating to witness the controversy aroused by Natural England's proposals to re-establish the white-tailed eagle as a breeding species in East Anglia. I am even more convinced that the project deserves wholehearted support after a recent visit to Wales.

The journey from my home involved an almost complete east–west traversal of the United Kingdom. Since the return leg was by a different route, in effect I made two separate transects of the whole country. During 1,170 kilometres I saw not a single large ground-nesting bird (discounting pheasants and red-legged partridges, which are non-native and reared in conditions of free-range chickens). The reason for this is simple. There is so little ground left.

We have versions of it, which looks green and pleasant, but it is not, on closer inspection, true countryside. It is space utilised and designed for pasture, crops or buildings, managed by machines, simplified by decades of chemical use and devoid of the kind of complexity that supports species such as grey partridge, lapwing and curlew.

We all know now the parlous statistics of farmland bird loss. They have resulted in what I would call a scorched-earth pattern of distribution. Birds like the tree sparrow or turtle dove (or the other wonderful grassland species named above) are reduced to pockets of abundance interspersed by large areas of nothing. The classic model for this type of range shrinkage is a bird banished by another century's change in landscape management, the corncrake. Valiant efforts by environmentalists have halted its chronic collapse, but it is nevertheless susceptible to total extinction if the conditions that have prevailed here recur across the entire range.

In short, the calamity suffered by this one bird is an example of what will happen to all large birds of agricultural country. My prediction is that without radical action to reverse the underlying causes, the entire suite of large and many smaller farmland birds will follow corncrakes into effective extinction in England by the twenty-second century. They will survive in Wales or Scotland and perhaps the eastern, western and northern fringes of England, but only with intensive support, specialised agri-environment schemes, large-scale reserve purchase and constant habitat manipulation.

I found another rationale for supporting the white-tailed eagle release scheme when I stopped off from my Welsh trip in north Derbyshire. Over the last thirty-five years I've watched changes in bird distribution on a patch of birch–oak woodland bordering heather moorland near my parents' home. True, I have gained common pheasant, Canada goose, great spotted woodpecker, long-tailed tit, jackdaw and rook, but over the decades I've witnessed the loss of breeding grey partridge, lapwing, common redshank, common snipe, dunlin, common sandpiper, cuckoo, tree pipit, whinchat, wheatear, ring ouzel, wood warbler and twite. My local patch represents in microcosm the other part of Britain's scorched-earth future – a huge across-the-board loss of bird diversity. But how does all this link to a reintroduction scheme for a raptor in Norfolk?

White-tailed eagles are large, dark, visceral, troubling, powerfully symbolic birds. They kill things. Large things. In the seventeenth century humans featured on its list of prey. Even modern environmentalists are worried about the impact. That for me is the point. If they are to be released they will require everyone to consider shuffling across a bit to make room. For far too long in this country we have only tolerated creatures that offer no challenge to our absolute dominance. If we are to secure a genuine future for birds then we must compromise our needs a tiny bit for theirs. What about a tithe of our landscape for nature: 85 per cent for us and, say, 15 per cent for the other eighty thousand species? That, at least, would be a start.

Birds, of course, are merely the final outcome, the largest, most visible and, for birders, the most charismatic product of an underlying ecosystem. The real engine room of biodiversity is a blend of the vegetation and the bio-luxuriance of its invertebrate populations. Birds are, if you like, already symbols of landscape. We need symbols now to try to get across the scorched-earth crisis that assails British nature.

People have got lost in arguments about the historicity of eagle presence in southern England. Which species was it? When were they here? Did they ever breed? We should perhaps set all those arguments aside for a moment because what seems indisputable is the strong proof that the species thrives very well now in lowland coastal environments adjacent to the Baltic and North Seas – an ecological zone of which East Anglia forms a part. Why can they have the bird, but we can't?

The presence of eagles in our region is not a return to the Anglo-Saxon past. It is a way of forging a new future, perhaps even a new relationship with nature. I can think of few better symbols for a different way of looking at the meaning, purpose and shared character of our landscapes than a white-tailed eagle.

5 September 2011

BUXTON, DERBYSHIRE

Rain had pressed down the heads of the bent grasses all around Lightwood so that the slopes looked to have been brushed and parted like wet hair. Each tiny ripe seed in the head of a bent stem was no more than a couple of millimetres long but its rusty colour had accumulated over the many millions of grasses so that in aggregate they turned the whole landscape a lovely soft rose. This warm note rhymed closely with the underparts on the migrant swallows, many of them this year's young, which had stopped to feed in the sunlit valley.

It looked like rich pickings. Heather flies were everywhere. They are soft-bodied, red-legged insects and are completely harmless, but they are slow-moving and have a tendency to dangle in vast swarms just around eye-level and easily become tangled in your hair or settle on your face. The swallows seemed to plunge in and out of these invertebrate pools at will.

Above the opposite slope little clusters of the birds chased one another in momentary ribbons of blue, the lines inscribing fantastically complex knots that all magically dissolved in an instant. Others rested on the heads of foxglove or settled in the tiny saplings of mountain ash. The rusty barbed wire was strung with swallows like blue-and-red beads. Then up they'd rise again to play or to sweep over the grasses. Wherever they found pockets of heather flies, so they slowed and hovered more intently, their wings outstretched and flickering, the tail opening and closing so that rows of white pearl spots blinked intermittently. Around this entire scene of birds and breeze and heather flies there was a wonderfully soothing envelope of twittering and burbling notes. It was warm. The sun shone. The birds were everywhere. There was such an air of luxury you had a feeling they could go on like this for weeks. The next day I went back to show them to my brother. We didn't see a single one.

8 September 2008

CLAXTON

All this week it has been ivy-flower time in our village. Down the lane the plant's strange extraterrestrial blooms cascade down the hedge in yellow-green terraces and are enveloped in a wonderful nebula of insect drone. The main buzz is produced by thousands of common wasps, and once I overcome that visceral childhood anxiety at the yellow and black stripes I can get really close.

Fortunately I'm no distraction to them. They are far more intent on roving across this vertical plane of old flower heads, cleaning up the surplus ivy pollen. In fact, the hedge's vast wall of proteins and minerals has inspired a feeding frenzy not just among the wasps but among a whole host of hoverflies, butterflies, flies and occasional bumblebees. Many of the insects are potential prey for the wasps, but much of the time all are completely focused upon the pollen. Briefly it seems that on this invertebrate Serengeti the lions shall lie down with the zebras.

Not everything in the hedge, however, is sweetness and light. The other common insect at this spot is the field digger wasp. If it is possible, it has a more intense predatory aura even than its vespine cousin. The body is compressed and its movements are redolent of restlessness and unpredictability.

Even the yellow and black parts are brighter, as if to signify a carnivore with unwavering instincts. Then one of them recovers a taste for something other than pollen. There is a shrill whining somewhere in the hedge as the eight wings of predator and prey vibrate against each other and against the foliage. Then it stops and the quiet cooperative hum of the ivy feast resumes.

Nabokov had his butterflies, but the authors of X-rated horror have their field digger wasps. Having secured her prey, the latter takes the comatose fly to her underground chamber, where she deposits her own egg as companion for the victim. The offspring then awaken to a world of total darkness and fresh meat.

13 September 2001

HARDLEY FLOOD, NORFOLK

At this small lake it was as if the birds had been allocated space according to species: the gadwall dabbling all together in one part, the shoveler sleeping in another and, in the middle, a compact raft of thirty-three great crested grebes. These birds were loafing in the evening sunlight, or rolling on to their white flanks to preen their belly feathers while others dived repeatedly for fish without obvious success. The whole group presented a seemingly inconsequential scene of random behaviours and I moved on after only a few minutes of scanning.

Yet as I did so I could not help recalling that in 1912 a young ornithologist looked out on a similar tableau at a series of reservoirs at Tring, Hertfordshire, and made scientific history. Julian Huxley had decided to sit down to study the courtship display of great crested grebes and, in a subsequent paper on the evolution of these behavioural patterns, he helped to establish ethology as an important branch of biological study. He showed the ways in which the elaborate postures adopted by displaying grebes had evolved out of much more functional forms of behaviour such as nest construction. However, it strikes me that an important part of Huxley's originality was simply to commit himself to observing what was already presumed to be a deeply familiar subject for a solid two weeks.

So much modern wildlife watching, by contrast, is a highly transient affair driven by an almost consumerist requirement for novelty. The main concern is often with identification without any deeper enquiry into aspects of behaviour. The recent explosion in the publication of natural-history books mainly reflects this preoccupation and, while it indicates a gain in breadth of knowledge, it may also imply a loss of depth.

I personally feel incapable of the level of patience shown by Eric Ennion, an artist who once thought nothing of spending seven hours at a Norfolk broad, lying in a punt under a canvas cover, studying and sketching a pair of black-necked grebes. It goes without saying that through such prolonged contact a deeper intellectual understanding is acquired, but one also senses that old-style naturalists like Ennion often gained a richer emotional empathy with their subjects.

My all-time favourite story of ornithological patience involves another Norfolk ornithologist, Willy Percy, an uncle of the celebrated wildlife writer Gavin Maxwell. Percy was a disputatious old curmudgeon who could argue furiously for hours about the colours of the soles to a song thrush's feet. However in our own age when ten minutes in a traffic jam is an eternity, Percy's eighty-seven days in succession at the side of a bittern's nest seems truly heroic. During the 1930s he spent more than a third of a year studying nesting bitterns. His extraordinary observations of this secretive heron species yielded a photograph sequence in which a bittern consumed an eel, which, if his calculations can be trusted, was virtually equal in length to the bird itself (about 70 centimetres). Eventually Percy published the fruits of his patient enquiries in a wonderfully eccentric book entitled *Three Studies in Bird Character*.

In this he revealed that during his long vigils in the Norfolk reedbeds he did occasionally get restless. One of his stranger forms of diversion was to dash from his boat out across the marsh towards a male bittern while it was booming (the name given to its resonant spring call). It was usually so distracted by the effort involved in its bizarre vocalisations that Percy was able to catch the bird before it could fly away.

18 September 2004

CLAXTON

Throughout much of September the heart of our village has been dominated by a wonderful pre-migration gathering of swallows and house martins, which run along the wires like a string of blue gems. I have an impression that, despite our awful summer, the season has been kind to both of these species and the group contains a high percentage of recently fledged young.

At their peak there were about a hundred and fifty and although each day sees the numbers dwindle, the residue still exudes an atmosphere of undiminished vitality. These highly communal species live within a permanent auditory bubble of buzzing calls and every now and then a male swallow breaks into that liquid burbling song which inspired the ancient Greeks to think of swallows as chattering gossips. To me, however, it has the same free, random structure as running water and I find it at once soporific and mesmerising.

Occasionally a sparrowhawk or a hobby – the latter is the only British falcon with the aerial agility to catch a swallow in flight – flashes across the sky and sends them all into a brief pulse of anxiety. The chattering intensifies and the birds hurl wildly outwards, before their agitation recedes and, like a settling of fine chaff, they come back in self-delighting spirals to captivate us once more.

As I enjoy their physical grace I start to reflect on what it is about blue birds that excites our fascination. One has only to think of our deep cultural attachments not only to swallows and martins, but also to the kingfisher and blue tit, to realise that it is almost a universal principle. Blue is rarely found in bird plumages, particularly amongst Europe's rather sober-toned avifauna, but I suspect that it is more than simply the magic of colour that determines our affections.

The swallow has always been the classic emblem of spring and, while our increasingly urbanised lifestyles have broken that common link with the bird and perhaps allowed the city-dwelling swift to replace it in that symbolic role, our affections remain deeply rooted. We have, for instance, no tradition of eating swallows and yet one need only recall that our other roof-nesting companion, the sparrow (and even its eggs!), was once widely consumed, to realise that smallness was no barrier to a creature's inclusion in our diet.

Yet far from being exploited, swallows were protected by strict taboos. In northern England people believed that harming the quintessential bird of the pastoral landscape would lead to the cows giving bloody milk or no milk at all. In Lancashire a parallel superstition held that maltreatment of swallows would cause the hens to stop laying. House martins may not have enjoyed such a high level of sanctity, but there is a similar sort of feeling for the species. People often speak of the birds nesting under their eaves as 'their' house martins, suggesting a deep almost proprietorial attachment. In Shakespeare's *Macbeth,* Banquo says of the 'temple-haunting martlet' that

> . . . no jutty, frieze,
> Buttress, nor coign of vantage, but this bird
> Hath made her pendent bed and procreant cradle.
> Where they most breed and haunt, I have observ'd
> The air is delicate.

Shakespeare's remark hints at a psychological affinity between humans and hirundines – the collective name for swallows and martins – that may stem from our very earliest origins. There was once a time when both the birds' ancestors and our own were troglodytes. Just as we sought the shelter of caves, so did the birds once attach their beautiful mud-built nests to the sides and in the fissures of natural rock faces. In fact, in parts of the Derbyshire dales, house martins can still be found clinging to their ancestral ways.

In prehistoric times one can presume that all three of us regularly shared exactly the same caves. And it is easy to imagine a degree of reciprocity in the home-sharing arrangement. Just as the birds would have readily hunted for flies and insects above the Palaeolithic midden, so one can well imagine Cro-Magnon woman enjoying the swallow's delightful brook-like song as she knapped her flint tools by the cave entrance. The long tradition of mutual trust between us was surely a key factor in the birds' gradual evolution from cave-dweller to eave- or barn-nesting species.

This switch probably began in the Tigris–Euphrates delta about eight thousand years ago, when we started to build our own substantial mudbrick dwellings, but that is a relatively short period in our shared domestic history. In fact, our relations with swallows and martins may be older than with almost any other species of bird. We may well have sheltered under the same roof for a hundred thousand years (ice ages excepted) and it is perhaps small wonder that when the birds relinquish their lease in the autumn it is a moment tinged with sadness.

19 September 2011

CLAXTON

As you looked over the marsh it seemed deeply anomalous that it was a sunlit September landscape but brutalised by gales that were pure December. The crowns of the trees flailed in a general north-easterly direction and the tall grasses running up the riverbank were bent to the ground. Yet some of the wider sights and sounds seemed to fit happily into both contexts. The rooks, for instance, shone like black flints on the fields, but with their low centre of gravity they hunkered down to the turf as they hammered and shovelled in the earth, and seemed entirely untroubled. There was also a winter quality to the grey heron's hoarse shout as it lumbered upstream. There was even something rather playful about the jackdaws, the way they swirled and flung themselves in great circular patterns against the gathering clouds. In that increasingly muddy sky they were like leaves swilled in dregs of a well-drained cup.

Yet it was hard to square the swallows with this place. Three or four of them swooped low across the River Yare, and were almost blown back with the force of the opposing airstream. Somehow they picked out narrow fissures in that cold bluff of wind, and slowly reached the other side. They then arced down over the fields, flying almost sideways, as if resting on one wing, using the right briefly as a flail to paddle against the blast.

By the time I'd turned for home the sun had gone. Rain started pounding down in diagonal sheets. Against the collar of my coat, which I raised to protect my glasses, it made a brittle sound like snapping twigs. When I got home I was completely soaked, cold trickles of water running down my shins. I thought finally of those blue birds. They weigh about 22 grams (less than 1 ounce), which works out roughly at a gram of wing muscle and sinew and hollow bone for every 450 kilometres of their forthcoming journey.

21 September 2010

Claxton

Garden cross spiders have a way of offending me – not because of any venomous predatory eight-legged creepiness, but because suddenly these exquisite creatures are so numerous, and I'm appalled that I barely notice until it seems their webs are draped on every bush. How could I be so unobservant? This year it was a fly that betrayed them. I happened to spot the aquamarine from the abdomen of a bluebottle, brilliant in the sunlight but all trussed up on a deathbed of silk.

A female cross spider enfolded this turquoise body and was sucking its juices. As I watched the feeding individual, I came to realise that cross-spider webs and their occupants were everywhere. The most captivating was the one owned by a gravid female being courted by her suitor.

As in many spiders, the garden cross exhibits a striking sexual dimorphism. He is perhaps as long but thinner, finer-bodied and with less than a quarter of her overall mass. Their courtship was an infinitely sensitive piece of choreography, conducted by the delicate touch of sixteen translucent legs and four palps (the short feelers at the front of the head), as well as vibrations transmitted through a tracery of silk.

He'd press forward, sampling the moods of his partner, proceeding with determination to satisfy his urges, then retreating almost as ardently. Although males can end up satisfying more than her sexual appetite, her desire to eat him is often exaggerated. This female finally got into a posture that enabled copulation, a process that is as strange in spiders as it is difficult to observe. He first transmits his sperm to his palps. She meanwhile presents herself, with four legs cocked mantis-like round her head, and offers to him a small aperture, called the epigyne, at the base of her abdomen. He moves in at super-speed as a mere blur to insert his palps at this vital point, and one registers their union only as an instantaneous flux of diaphanous limbs.

22 September 2008

CLAXTON

At the foot of the lane, the leggy overgrown limbs of the hawthorn hedge have become so smothered by bramble you could easily think this was just a blackberry bush five metres tall. It cascades down its hawthorn superstructure in a great tent of purple fruit and red-spined leaves. And in late afternoon it is as if all the summer in our parish has mustered at this spot for one last stand.

A sweet black juice tide seems to be draining down with gravity slowly to its base. As it descends, so a variety of moulds catch many of the rotting fruits. Any that are left and even those furred up with mould set a feast for a vast swarm of insects.

My favourite, the one I've stood here an hour to capture on camera, is the comma butterfly. The closed wings, the side with the telltale white punctuation mark, are the exact tannin brown of old oak leaves. But when those ragged-edged wings open they seem almost to burst into flame. They are so bright, in fact, that my camera seems unable to capture the colour.

Using mere words, I would say it was the 300-million-year-old fire of hot coals, Carboniferous orange.

After an hour of virtual stillness – with the warm glow on my neck from the sun, the occasional tickling scamper of a fly – I feel myself becoming a part of this landscape. At one point a common sympetrum dragonfly takes advantage of that outstretched hand to land and sun itself. Moments later, a flesh-fly replaces it and I can see how the flat-bottomed pads at the end of its six legs glue to the human skin and hairs like the suckers on the toes of tropical frogs.

As that hand and its pen move across the page to write these words, so the fly moves with it. And, nonchalantly, it turns directly to the sun, the better to catch the last warmth.

24 September 2007

Claxton

Just as I was pouring the coffee I spotted it – a strange, hunched presence on the lawn that immediately had me dashing for the telescope and tripod. At sixty times magnification the sparrowhawk's head looked immense, its acid-yellow eye lasering the space between us like a searchlight.

It was a beautiful young male, the mantle feathers fringed with rufous, the crown circled by a white tonsure, and I also noted how the exact same feather on each side (the innermost greater covert) had a white spot with identical shape. These are the insignia of youth – it is a mere four and a half months since those yellow eyes burst open – and so too are the heart-shaped spots on its chest, which I could count with unusual precision. Thirty-three in all.

A fid of meat draped over the right edge of its bill was the exact colour of the blackbird's legs, now stripped down to red sinew with dangling feet. Young and inexperienced he may be, but he was more than a match for an adult female blackbird and had dismantled her in customary fashion, meticulously laying bare the breast, whose featherless skin was the purplish tone of a fresh bruise. Methodically he hauled out the glistening muscle ball that was her gizzard and I was surprised to see him eating this before all the breast meat was gone. Even more surprising was the sudden appearance of an intact snail from among the part-digested paste.

The mustard-coloured seeds I could see adhering to the snail proved to be from the fruits of our pheasant-berry bush and from these visceral details I could construct the blackbird's last moment. Hauling at the fruits, she was momentarily distracted from the bullet-like shadow descending upon her. Yet entwined in her death is new life. Those seeds will pass through the sparrowhawk gut and, in time, if his droppings fall in some propitious spot, from them will spring more pheasant-berry bushes that will bear fruits beloved of blackbirds.

26 September 2005

CLAXTON

At present it is cranefly season for the spiders in our house. There is not a web throughout the property that doesn't sport dismembered wings or other assorted daddy-long-leg body parts. (In fact, the chitinous remains are so embarrassingly abundant that it has inspired a selective weeding of the webs themselves.) Worst of all are the whole cranefly carcasses trussed up like rolls of brisket in a net of silk, but left uneaten, presumably as a spidery insurance against lean times.

The other day I happened to be looking at precisely the spot on the lawn where one of these weird, gangly insects first saw the light of day. The forelimbs emerged like disembodied antennae. Slowly the cranefly levered out its tubular body. Although fully developed it had emerged from the pupa case looking like a half-formed blob, the limbs, wings and body only disentangling in the warmth of the sunlight. The way it bulbed out of the earth reminded me of that moment in the film *Terminator 2* when we first catch a glimpse of the shape-shifting robot, curled naked in the foetal posture.

However, it is the only area of similarity between the relentless terminator and a cranefly, because the insect seems to have the most casual grasp on life of any creature I know. Yesterday I was given a graphic demonstration. Noticing one on the path I tried to put it out of harm's way and, having picked it up, it took flight, but not before it relinquished one of its legs to my safekeeping.

Possibly the adult creature's haplessness is a way of lulling us into a false complacency. That way we overlook the fact that in larval form the cranefly is itself a relentless devourer of crops and, until the advent of chemical pesticides, was a major scourge known as the leatherjacket.

OCTOBER

3 October 2011

Claxton

The perversity of Norfolk pronunciation, which somehow contrives 'wind-am' out of Wymondham and 'haze-bre' from Happisburgh, has worked its wonderful economy in our village. You might look at the map and call it Peascod Lane but we know the track linking us to Ashby St Mary as 'Pusky' Lane. Above it the ozone was deepest blue and the hedges on both sides of Peascod trapped and stewed the July sunlight so that you would have sworn it was midday in summer. Summer, perhaps, except for the silence that was so intense I could hear the crepitation of wings as red admiral butterflies dashed from one patch of flowering ivy to the next. The ivy's globes of lime green were on one side and down the other were thick purple boughs of drooping sloes, while underfoot was the ground meal from crushed acorns so that Peascod was one long avenue of colour, fruit and fertility.

It was dead silent but it was the perfect context to bring out the subtlety of dark bush crickets. They have sung to us all summer, but now the landscape has lapsed into autumn quietude you can hear these fabulous insects all the clearer. It is the thinnest, driest of songs, a rustling together of the male's tiny crêpe wings, a soothing buzz that somehow contrives to be fainter now than it was two months ago. It is as if the miniature hooks arranged along the wing edge that produce the sound have worn away over the bush crickets' summer of music. What we have is a residual autumn purr. It is still the signature sound of our village, especially at dusk when we take our increasingly nocturnal evening stroll. As we walk the bush crickets still bow their tiny notes, singing to the pencil line of orange on the western horizon, and to the blurry veil of moisture hovering over the beck and to the tawny owls, whose own songs pierce and arc across the dome of Claxton's night sky.

5 October 2009

CLAXTON

The dry summer in our area probably accounts for the mixed fortunes of blackberries this autumn. My favourite patches have been largely barren but my younger daughter, chief picker in recent weeks, has had no trouble finding superb black bowlfuls with her friends. (She has been cautious about revealing the exact source of their harvests and also where they scrumped the apples that went into the mixed fruit pies.)

Many of our local lanes are tiered with vast rambling mounds of bramble. Who knows how long they might have stood there? Unlike trees, we tend not to project any sense of age or dignity on to anything as small as a shrub or plant. Yet some of these dusty, crab-backed palisades of spike must be truly ancient.

Bramble has a significant place in the British landscape. Really well-established mounds are in effect miniature patches of wilderness. No human eye, let alone human hand, has penetrated those walls of spine-ribbed leaf. Their dark secrets fill me with a rich sense of mystery.

The sounds of rabbit-scamper, or the ripping noise of spine-raked pheasant wings when one bursts forth, even just the night-time purr of the dark bush crickets, which really love bramble patches, serve to deepen my sense of curiosity. I sometimes think about cutting a transect through favourite stands, to give some sort of access to these bramble secrets. Yet ultimately would it not violate what I love most about them? Setting aside for one moment their great gifts to the human eye each spring, and to our dining tables each autumn, we should recognise that brambles are among the last undiscovered realms in our countryside, and we should encourage them all the more for that reason.

8 October 2007

COMBS EDGE, DERBYSHIRE

Suddenly from the last rowan on the hillside rose a long-winged, lean blackbird-like thrush with a call that sounded like stone upon stone. It was a ring ouzel and as this shy bird speared its way to the ridge on the moorland edge, it also drilled down through thirty-five years of memory to my first ever encounter with the species. It was April 1972. I was twelve.

Initially I had no idea what I was seeing. I was separated from the mystery bird, a female, by a steep-sided clough above Buxton. After twenty minutes' close scrutiny a great wave of excitement began to rise within as its identity eventually dawned on me. I now understand the exact constituents of that thrill.

One part was matching the features of the living creature to the two-dimensional illustrations in *The Observer's Book of Birds* – the key detail separating it from its relative, the blackbird, was a quarter-moon patch of cream upon its chest. The other part was a realisation that those twenty to thirty cream feathers implied a wholly separate genetic history and lifestyle. And in the ring ouzel's millennial-long journey through time, this was the first moment that I personally had intercepted it.

It's a moment I still cherish. In fact, I'd go so far as to say that this experience is one of the great gifts to humankind, because within it lies an appreciation of our own unique identity. Simultaneously we are made aware of how we share with other species the same neighbourly time and space. Aldous Huxley suggested that this sense of communion with our fellow-creatures had given rise to half the poetry in the English canon. I suspect the poets are proclaiming what we all feel and what I felt when that ring ouzel rose from the rowan tree. How miraculous that we are all here, now, in this one small place.

10 October 2005

CLAXTON

It was one of those strokes of fortune that bless naturalists about twice a year. A kingfisher speared down the dyke towards us and pulled up on a post within touching distance. The bird was so close we could appreciate the subtle texture to the colours creating the more typical if momentary kingfisher flash of electric blue and flame orange. (In fact, the underparts graded from white on the chin to terracotta on the chest. The blue back, meanwhile, actually seemed rather dull, while the bill tip was a sort of mud colour.) As the kingfisher bobbed its head you could also see the gills working on a tiddler clasped in its beak. But what struck me most of all was the bird's calmness – the way that it took in our identities, processed the risks and vanished, all without a hint of alarm.

It was a week before I could appreciate the full significance of that encounter. I was heading to the dustbin when another blue bird, this one the blue-brown of a male sparrowhawk, swooped with lazy stealth up beneath the yellowing skirts of a sycamore. The movement was so smooth I felt sure I was the only one who had spotted his entry. But no. As the sparrowhawk blended into the foliage, so a mistle thrush took flight skywards and away. There was no panic, just momentary comprehension and escape.

I realised that there is seldom terror among wild creatures. There is rather, among the fearless trees and grasses, a perpetual dance by predator and prey – spider and fly, hawk and thrush, man and crow – that is choreographed by their mutual perception. The world is one glorious vigilant eye and in order to succeed the hunter must find a blind spot in that enveloping sphere of watchfulness.

11 October 2002

The lanes around Claxton are now a blaze of colour. Amid the remaining full-blown greenery of the hedgerow foliage are dead stems of hogweed with heads of brown seed, and tufts of forlornly yellowed grasses still clambering upwards to the light. Some hawthorn leaves are turning sepia at the edges, while along the road the bushes are sprayed randomly with clusters of scarlet berries. A host of tortoiseshell and peacock butterflies wanders back and forth down the corridors of warm air, their bright wings rhyming with every hue in the wider hedgerow.

These glorious insects are a last reminder of summer, but today we are after one of the classic totems of autumn – bramble bushes. Although they all look similar to a botanically untrained eye, British brambles comprise about four hundred micro-species that are separated by tiny differences in structure, colour, fruit and flavour. Our ancestors were not aware of these technical matters, but each region had its own name for the plant – black begs in Yorkshire, black kites in Cumbria, black boyds in Scotland and doctor's medicine in Somerset.

That last piece of West Country vernacular refers to the fact that brambles were once believed to have health-giving properties. The plant was said to cure digestive disorders, and in the seventeenth century the *London Pharmacopoeia* declared blackberry cordial a natural restorative. More primitive was a belief that a person suffering from rheumatism and other diseases could be cured if made to walk under a bramble arch rooted on either side.

Today we are in pursuit of a different kind of blackberry magic – their great panicles of lustrous fruits. Blackberry picking has a long pedigree. A Neolithic man pulled from the submerged clays on the Essex coast was found to have blackberry seeds still in his stomach. My daughters respond to these ancient impulses and soon come to resemble a pair of hunter-gatherers.

With mouths stained purple, they forage deep into the thickest bushes, clamouring excitedly when they find a particularly rich patch and oblivious to the nettle stings and bramble claw marks.

We are not the only creatures involved in the free-for-all. This year has seen a particularly rich crop and great bunches have caused the brambles' limbs to sag with the burden. All around these udders of purple fruit is a swarm of insects: small iridescent green flies that I never notice at any other time of the year, plump-bodied bluebottles and wasps intent on a final orgy of sweetness before the frosts kill them. The ground is splattered with purple bird droppings that are filled with the hard indigestible seeds, reminding us that blackberries also prime the engines of bird migration.

Very soon we have acquired all the skills of our Neolithic ancestors, stripping the outermost fruit first, then in sequence up each side of the panicle. We test each one for that exact combination of firmness and soft give typical of a really ripe berry. We leave those with a grey down of mildew and the unripe raspberry-coloured fruits with an eye to a future harvest. But, in truth, we know our blackberrying days are over for another year. By Michaelmas the devil is said to render them inedible – by urinating on them.

15 October 2012

CLAXTON

If you want an object lesson in humility then I recommend you go out in the early morning or evening, when the sun is at a low angle, and examine any length of fencing. Glistening from every link in the chain is a gossamer of spiders' webs. In fact, some fences here are so smothered there are actually two structures – one of galvanised metal but another infinitely finer, continuous tissue of silk. And don't be deceived by its ephemeral nature: gram for gram, spider silk is stronger than tensile steel.

You quickly realise that spiders are everywhere. One estimate suggests 2.5 million per hectare. We might well hold the title deeds, but this is not our land. It belongs to spiders. Or, at least it did, because the real era of the spider's web is the cusp of late summer and early autumn. We now live largely amid the ruins of this year's arachnid dynasty but evidence of its existence, all that dust-laden silk, is still a remarkable phenomenon.

My favourite is the orb-web, which is made by one of our commonest species, the garden cross spider, itself a glorious gem with sparkling white markings on a background that varies from soft grey-brown right through to brightest conker chestnut. Most individual webs of this species that I've counted have around twenty to twenty-five radials per web with a comparable number of ever-decreasing circles, each one beautifully spliced into the circumference of the last. However, I did find one that had thirty-six radials and thirty-seven circumferences. It meant that in order to complete her web the spider in question had linked her silk lines 1,332 times to make the full glistening sphere. She does it mainly at night purely by touch and yet by morning the thing is always the same Platonic model of perfection, gilded often by microscopic beads of dew. The earliest spiders to have appeared on earth arose in the Devonian four hundred million years ago, so think how old that form is. When you see a spider's web you are looking at a work of art whose design was worked out before our species or even any kind of mammal had ever existed.

19 October 2009

Claxton

There were swallows over the trees. That lambent downward quick beat of their wings, which is such a signature of swallow flight, already seemed an anachronism against this autumn landscape, with its slow swirl of white-glinting gulls and the heavy crows battering towards the woods.

The naturalist Max Nicholson once wrote something I always try to remember on seeing swallows, that truly they are not birds of the land; rather their primary habitat is a thin layer of sky that lies just above the earth's surface. Swallows are before everything citizens of air.

To disentangle them in our minds like this from any association with terra firma also helps us to recall their international character. For they inhabit the same air layer regardless of what lies beneath. The only secondary requirement is that it is warm enough to billow upwards to them the insects on which they feed. The birds that flicker now over Norfolk could be over a Moroccan wadi next month or above the acacias of northern Nigeria a month later. Come Christmas and they may be riffling through the hot eddies off the Angola highlands. One wonders if swallows can taste the different places in the flavour of the insects. Warm and dark, perhaps, over East Anglian loams, but bitter and astringent as they float over the Saharan ergs. This invertebrate connection between place and swallow brings us back to Nicholson's remark, because while they may not be land birds, they are birds of different lands. The insects they eat over the Sahelian savannah or the Congolese rainforest are transmuted via the swallow's respiratory system into hirundine feather and muscle. So in a sense they are birds of land but of every land that they cross. I propose that each autumn we have a special swallow day on which we celebrate this enamel blue miracle and then we might recall the vast oneness of our planet.

20 October 2008

CLAXTON

Almost every week this year I've run a moth trap in my garden. It is essentially a bright light suspended over a box, into which moths fall and then pass the night, until I can liberate them the following day. Intermittently I have to perform a task that is one half guilty horror, the other half wonder and astonishment.

The screw-in socket to the bulb gradually fills with a residue of dead insects – not moths, but flies, tiny wasps and minuscule beetles – and I'm obliged to clean it out. On to a piece of white paper I gently shake out the collateral damage of moth trapping: the unsuspecting, blameless creatures, which, lured to the bulb, are instantly incinerated by its intense heat. When they are finally dislodged from the socket I am confronted with hundreds of tiny but perfectly preserved and completely unknown neighbours, whose futile passing I cannot even memorialise with a name. One fly nestled in my ten-pence-piece-sized spread of corpses shines like glass and is the colour of the eyes in a peacock's upper-tail coverts. Through a hand-lens I am confronted by an array of detail: complex mouth parts, intricately segmented legs, abdomens bristling with fine hairs. Yet all this information doesn't serve as a revelation. In a way, it only deepens the sense of mystery and confusion. What does it all mean?

The lives and individual deaths of these tiny insects probably surround us at every step we take, and yet we seldom if ever notice. In fact, one slightly heavier breath and my meditation ends as all this invertebrate mystery is puffed away. These tiny creatures are part of the very fabric of our parish life. In transmuted form they are the summer-long songs of birds, they are the fish in the dykes, the otter I saw this summer and the vixen thrumming away over the dusk fields. They are the adult dragonfly I saw yesterday evening, glistening silvery somehow through the shadows down the track by the gate, out to the wide marsh.

24 October 2005

CLAXTON

At the moment around our village, the roads are an ecological unit all of their own. The mangled remains of pheasants greet the driver almost every few hundred metres. But, if anything, the number of carcasses seems to have tailed off in recent months. During the earlier part of the year the males, hardly smart creatures at the best of times, seem to have just sex on their tiny brains and become extraordinarily susceptible to road accidents. Spring in Norfolk is truly a time of love and death for cock pheasants.

The most recent dramatic increase in casualties has involved squirrels and no doubt the summer crop of inexperienced juveniles has borne the brunt, weeding them down to the streetwise before winter arrives.

Of course, not everything is in the debit column. You swing round a corner and invariably a magpie or crow, which are almost never casualties themselves, rises nonchalantly from the latest bloody mess. But the largest clean-up operations must happen under cover of darkness and it always brings me an ironic smile to reflect that what the local pheasant-shooting community takes with one hand by directly culling foxes, they give with the other by maintaining a roadside takeaway service for their enemy-in-chief.

One of my neighbours, a man with a Gilbert White-style passion for the telling local detail, kept an annual inventory of roadkills during the 1960s. For three years he logged every bird he found on a two-mile stretch of the local highway. His annual average was 159 birds, with a full species range of twenty, including a depressing number of swallows and house martins.

To give you some sense of its implications at a national level and working on a figure of 100,000 miles as a stab at the total length of our main roads, I calculate that in the last forty years we have mown down something in the region of 320 million birds.

31 October 2011

CLAXTON

We think of winter as a season largely without harvest but it's not strictly the case. This morning I picked its first fruits with a flock of fieldfares, those northern thrushes that come to this country from Scandinavia and the Baltic area. They flew in a wide arc across a peerless blue sky, then landed in the hawthorn bushes by the beck. They sat proud of the canopy, upright and alert, while their clattering contact calls piled up all around them. On this morning, in that sunlight, for the first time this season they looked more wonderful than ever, as if they had just been freshly minted.

Fieldfares were actually a real harvest at one time because people used to trap and eat them in massive numbers. They are said to be delicious. There is a beautiful Roman mosaic discovered near Ingolstadt in Germany that dates to about AD 150, which depicts hunters trapping the birds. Thrush catching was a very important tradition in that region and only ceased during the early twentieth century. Some historians suggest that at its peak more than a million fieldfares were killed annually in eastern Prussia alone.

Today our fieldfare crop is different. One part is their glorious colour. The underwings are a sparkling grey and about the same shade as sunlit money. Above and below they are brown but these are subtle browns that mix tones of deep earth with wild fruit. Fieldfares are always surrounded by a palisade of high-strung chakking notes that have a quality of defiance. In truth, each of these wonderful creatures is a small flag of life in a dead season. A friend once told me how his terminally ill mother was given final comfort by an image of fieldfares sailing in that indefatigable true-winged way they have, straight into the jaws of a biting northerly. It seems to me that there are few personal gifts from nature richer than that.

NOVEMBER

5 November 2007

CLAXTON

Along the lane to the marsh I invariably stop on most autumn mornings at the spot where the hedge is smothered in ivy. The waxy leaves are so dense and close-fitting that for thirty metres they give it the appearance of a short green tunnel, rather than a line of vegetation.

The underlying hedge is composed of field maple and hawthorn, but it is largely invisible apart from sections where the trees upthrust their long fingers of new growth. At one point the branches of a small oak have also broken through the ivy mass, reaching upwards for the sun like outstretched arms. But its leaves are now scrolled up and covered in mildew, giving them a milky, sickly pallor.

A few weeks ago the whole section was a mass of bright lime ivy flowers, literally buzzing with insect life. Yet the red admirals, whose blood-coloured wings brought a note of high autumn to proceedings, are elsewhere now, and most of the other insects are all gone. The dominant sound is the faintly menacing whine of wasps, which move about the old flowers with that characteristic mix of airy reticence and predatory sweep.

The ivy flowers themselves, which were the main attraction for all the flies, hoverflies, social wasps and ichneumons, are almost over and the freshly budding green berries on the old heads look like minuscule sputniks freshly docked among the foliage. One of the last signs of the ivy's late flourish is the old pollen-bearing stamens that have fallen off and gathered in rows along abandoned spiders' webs, tricking them out in filaments of faded green.

The place is still full of fascination for me but that rich deep invertebrate drone has grown thin and is overlain at intervals by the calls of redwing and fieldfare and the sad sibilant notes of meadow pipits. All are winter visitors, and as I leave I realise the spot has acquired the weird, ambiguous air of a freshly built mausoleum.

6 November 2006

CLAXTON

After more than a month of unseasonal mildness, winter seemed to come to the Yare in one great rush. As I looked upstream along the valley, the cloud was towering into the sky in an advancing black horde. As a prelude to the downpour, the vegetation went into a gale-lashed frenzy as if it were desperate to escape the inevitable onslaught.

There were three basic notes in the music of the south-west wind. The quietest, a sort of brushed hiss, came from the grass. Soft and insistent, it kept to ankle level and I had to strain to pick it out from the wider soundscape. The second and most pleasing contribution rose from the long bed of phragmites reeds, which were pressed over by the wind to an angle of about 60 degrees from the ground. The flat blade-like leaves tugged constantly at their stems, and seemed to be reaching out to the north-east in a plea for mercy. Yet there was some comfort in the song of these reedbeds, which rustled soothingly like a generous flow of meal on to a stone floor.

There was, however, no consolation in the noise above me. The trees, a line of thick-trunked poplars, had been stripped of leaves, and the wind worked the bare twigs, the branches and even the trunks. The result was a dark booming bass sound, like the relentless impact of water upon shattered rock. Then came the first rain and instantly the rich green tones in the far landscape withered to shades of grey or black. Finally, I too was engulfed. The scribbled lines in my notebook bled one into the other, and the words that I offer you now melted slowly in the winter rain.

12 November 2012

BLACKWATER CARR, NORFOLK

Just after I planted the onions on our allotment I started to find new excavations all along my neat rows. Sifting through the soil I came across a secondary sowing – of acorns. Almost daily for the last month I've also seen these renegade gardeners, passing repeatedly across the skies with that strangely faltering flight pattern. They belong to the species W. H. Hudson called the 'British bird of paradise', the European jay.

It is strange that Western society has such a downer on corvids, to which family jays belong, because they are truly the birds with the deepest work ethic. Every autumn the average jay plants five thousand acorns to retrieve as food in the winter. I'm a direct beneficiary of this avian providence because I have a single magnificent oak on my marsh at Blackwater Carr. About a century ago an acorn somehow made its way hundreds of metres across the intervening ground from the nearest parent tree, and came to rest in the dark peat of my land. I can easily imagine who was the delivering 'midwife'.

Jays are impressive for their labours, but what about the nutcrackers that are spread right across Eurasia? Each is thought to cache a hundred thousand seeds, but retrieves only about a quarter of these in the subsequent months. In North America the scrub, pinyon and Steller's jays are all avid tree-farmers and often specialise in favoured species. Even the blue jay, whose slaughter Atticus Finch licensed in the novel *To Kill a Mockingbird,* would be a bird widely approved in most American pulpits, if only the ministers knew what an honest industrious creature it really is. One blue jay was recorded to plant one hundred thousand beechnuts in one month. Perhaps the best way to rehabilitate the crow family is to promote a vision of these wonderful birds at a hemispheric level. They are the great keepers of the northern forests and are busy now husbanding that vast carbon-rich landscape in its millennial journey north as climate change begins to take hold.

15 November 2009

CLAXTON

Decoy Carr still has canopy enough to allow just a dingy yellow-green light that emphasises its air of claustrophobia. Winter frosts will soon scythe down the choking vegetation from between the alder and birch trees but for now the path is entangled by dead stems of nettles. Spikes of hemp agrimony or burdock stand as upright as when they first grew. Yet now the stems are brown, kiln-dry and lifeless. The burdock, in customary fashion, manages to hook one claw into me and instantly my whole jumper front is claggy with a dozen seed heads. I have to stop completely to rip them off one by one. Even then those devilish hooks cling to my fingertips. At least the entanglement of Decoy Carr tells me that no one has been there since my last visit in summer. It confers a sense of ownership and in that hour-long illusion of possession I find the wood all the more enchanting. Its highlight comes quietly breezing in. Suddenly a belt of trees is infused with a thin tissue of bird notes. They are long-tailed tits, each one keeping connection with its neighbour through a perpetual ricochet of contact calls. The species is so intensely social, one set of offspring even helping their parents to raise the next generation, that to talk of a single long-tailed tit is a contradiction in terms. This loose net of birds before me, as well as their enveloping gauze of sound, feels and behaves like a single organism. Yet in truth I hardly see it: a blur of pink, a momentary trace of white, a flurry of wings. It is all so intangible and yet they are so emphatically here. Each single dry single-syllable call proclaims vigour and certainty. For the minutes that they are present those nine-gram birds with their less-than-one-gram hearts possess the landscape completely. Then they are gone and I find myself, as one should in a wood, back at the place where I started.

15 November 2010

CLAXTON

The river was swollen, the paths sodden and slippery and a brutal rain-laden north-easterly, carrying heavy grey skies with it, sailed through the Yare Valley. The wind bellied out among the phragmites at the river edge and I was amazed to see a pair of stonechats, tiny thrush-relatives, bending and swaying, flexing their tails and flicking wings to compensate for this movement, yet clinging hard to the reed tops.

They are delightful birds, with a sweet rounded shape and large innocent eyes centred in a large head. She is so drably mottled that one tends to fix on her mate: his black face offset by a white collar and the soft rusty tone of the belly that seems a colour deeply apt to the season, matching shades within the reeds themselves or the distant oaks. For these are winter birds in our parish and depart in spring.

What I love most about stonechats, which are almost invariably in pairs, is their unobtrusiveness. They are virtually silent, never fly far, do little dramatic, but flick from bush top to fence post and on across a landscape, dipping now and then to pick up insects or spiders. Occasionally something troubles them and they muster to produce this quiet tacking note, which they accompany with much wing flicking, but it's as if they wished to raise the alarm yet somehow not make a fuss.

There is something grand about so small an animal that rides out winter here. The American author Ralph Waldo Emerson celebrated this capacity in his poem 'The Titmouse'. It describes his own winter walk in heavy snow and his encounter with a small bird, whose example provided him with what he called the antidote of fear. 'Here was this atom in full breath/ Hurling defiance at vast death.' The stonechat has another strategy. It manages somehow to find the interstices not only in our attention, but also those tiny creases in winter's dreary expanse that lead eventually to spring.

17 November 2008

CLAXTON

This month our village has been invaded by a mob of fieldfares, which come here in winter from eastern Europe and Scandinavia. The exact number in the area is difficult to establish partly because of the strange mechanics of fieldfare behaviour as they harvest the berries on the hawthorn hedgerows.

The bird's personality is an intriguing mix of timidity and almost threatening boldness. As you walk down the hedge the fieldfares secreted in those bushes suddenly burst out in a manner that suggests almost desperate panic. The audible ripping of feathers against thorny twigs is so loud one also imagines that extrication is often a rather painful process. The leaving is accompanied by vocalisations that have a raw, mechanical, clattering quality. Then no sooner have they risen up than the birds recover their nerve and return to the same trees, but just a fraction further along the lane. This looping flight-and-return pattern is repeated several times down a single hedgerow. The bit I cherish most is the way that fieldfares convert retreat into attack. They don't so much fly back. They spear down upon the trees and at the last minute surf back up into the top branches, white underwings gleaming and chest pushed out like a prize cock in a gesture of defiance. And all this amid a great deal of those rattling cries.

There is something wildly robust about fieldfares that fits the season exactly. At their best, in fact, they are a distillation of the whole winter. The black chest streaks mimic the bare thorn. The wider suffusion of burnt ochre is an exact match for the oak's last leaves, or the light at sunset. The colour across the head and down the lower back is the same blending of grey and blue in the cold sky. When their jostling silhouettes crown the treetops at dusk they seem like a defiant gesture – a waved fist – signifying life's continuance in the midst of decay.

19 November 2005

SEXTON WOOD, NORFOLK

I remember the occasion primarily for its grisliness. Even the winter wood in which it took place – the skeletal pattern of the branches, the iron-hard grip of frost upon the earth and the flaring low-angled winter sunlight – seemed all at one with the stark character of the moment. At the side of the track I was suddenly aware of a brown shadow, no more than a momentary presence, slipping instantly from sight. At the point where it left the ground I could work out the identity of the mysterious shape from an array of circumstantial evidence left behind.

It was a female sparrowhawk and she had been feeding on a newly caught wood pigeon. Already the prey was reduced to a random orbit of plucked feathers around a carcass that had been sliced down to its breast bone. Grisly it may have been but it was a perfect illustration of the hunting prowess of this remarkable little bird of prey, because the pigeon was probably twice the weight of its captor.

A male sparrowhawk, sometimes as little as 110 grams (4 ounces), is our smallest bird of prey by weight. *Mosca* ('fly'), an old Italian name for it, was where we derived our own word 'musket', which originally referred to a crossbow bolt and then, of course, to the early form of firearm. I suppose our linguistic borrowings from the sparrowhawk were a compliment of sorts, but they captured little of the sheer hunting élan with which it compensates for lack of weight. Its typical modus operandi involves a lightning strike completely without warning.

Shaped like a soft-nosed bullet, often very low to the ground, it will suddenly flip over a hedge to take any bird on the other side unfortunate enough to have been unsighted by the intervening shelter. Nor are sparrowhawks put off by human proximity. I routinely see them hunting in front of the car down the road, or look into the garden and suddenly spot the telltale low-level blur vanish into the bottom of bushes previously occupied by sparrows. Its willingness to hunt around our homes brings the scene of carnage described in my opening paragraph to the kitchen window. People can become very distressed when they see garden birds – *their* blackbirds, sparrows and thrushes – suddenly struck down before their eyes.

Some have taken it one stage further and elevated these scenes of domestic violence into the basis for a campaign. A small pressure group called Songbird Survival has been lobbying for the reduction of sparrowhawks for several years, arguing that the recent declines in birds such as song thrush, skylark, tree sparrow and bullfinch are attributable to the predation inflicted by this bird of prey.

It is certainly the case that sparrowhawks have significantly increased in recent decades, especially when compared with the population slump of the 1960s and 1970s. The birds of prey were severely affected by organochlorine pesticides, but with the withdrawal of these chemicals the raptors recovered, only now to have suffered a second inexplicable reversal in the last decade, with a national fall in numbers of 20 per cent, a figure that is doubled in our eastern region.

Despite this downturn in sparrowhawk fortunes, Songbird Survival has maintained its campaign to have the bird's numbers further reduced, although with little prospect of success. The one insuperable barrier to their project is the lack of evidence to substantiate their key complaint against sparrowhawks. All the studies show that there was not a dramatic increase in the birds that sparrowhawks eat during the period of their own slump, nor has there been any comparable decline in numbers of blue tits and great tits, two important prey items, in the years of the sparrowhawk's subsequent rise.

While it is true that birds such as song thrush and tree sparrow have declined, all evidence indicates that these reductions are related to habitat loss resulting from intensive agriculture. A group like Songbird Survival is fascinating not for what it tells us about the true state of affairs with our birds, but for what it says about us. Blaming the sparrowhawk is a classic case of creating a scapegoat – that poor reviled beast that serves as a lightning conductor for our feelings of disappointment, frustration and anger when things are not as they should be.

Pinning the blame on one often defenceless element simplifies the emotional and intellectual challenge. It frees us from any unwelcome search for a complex truth, particularly when that quest requires that we look within. The unpalatable fact is that all of us, at some level, are implicated in the loss of our songbirds. The prolonged British drive to ever-more intense levels of agricultural production, triggered largely by the public appetite for ever-cheaper food, is the real cause.

Unpicking the intractable social knot will involve complex political action and negotiation at the highest level. How much simpler it seems to pick up your gun, walk out of the door, and solve your problems with a left and a right.

19 November 2007

CLAXTON

When I say I can smell winter, I'm not just talking about that curious astringent sensation at the bridge of your nose when you breathe in the sharp ice air. A north-easterly in our village brings with it a long, slewed line of vapour from the sugarbeet factory, and it spreads among the houses a stink that is one part pleasure, but two parts nausea.

When I say that this morning I heard the winter arrive, I'm not referring to my finger tapping at the mercury, nor the high clear notes of redwing in the garden. As I crossed the lawn they were panicked into flight from our holly trees and released a sound like air held under high pressure and escaping from a valve. Nor do I mean the delicious crunchy racket when I walk the wood almost completely bare of leaves. Today, rather, it was the gentle honking from a skein of Bewick's swans, which crossed the sky to the west. How extraordinary that this reassuring murmur of contact notes will have enveloped them like a bubble all the way from northern Russia.

When I say that I can now see winter, I'm not thinking of the way clouds appear denser at this time of year and congeal towards evening, pressing down upon the horizon and squeezing the last light to a glorious band of pale magenta. Instead I have in my mind's eye that huge female peregrine. She sat on a gate in the middle of the field. She did almost nothing, except the head rotated those huge eyes, larger than my own, across the fields. Every duck, goose or wader was potential prey, and it seemed as if the mood of this whole landscape was made tangible, each strand of the fabric ultimately converging in that falcon on its post. Any moment now she could just fly upwards and unleash upon us all the stark and beautiful madness of a snowstorm.

20 November 2006

CLAXTON

It was a shaft of light that showed the way. A pinhole in the cloud let through one intense beam that fired down obliquely across the fields and into the ragged canopy. It scythed its way down through the yellows and browns to leave a small globe of brightness on the woodland floor. Among the mounds of sunlit sweet-chestnut leaves was the litter from a thousand nut cases. Yet every one had been picked clean – presumably by squirrels, mice and pigeons, perhaps even by rooks – and there was not a single jewel nut for my troubles.

Almost self-consciously at first I began to scuff the leaves as I walked away for that delicious crunchy music. I soon recovered my taste for the sport and by the end I was completely lost, sending up great cascades of leaves as high as I could boot them. It reminded me of my conker expeditions in childhood, when we'd go to the woods in search of prize-fighters. In Derbyshire there can only have been a bumper crop once every five years, when there were so many even an upfolded jumper couldn't hold the whole rich harvest. Most years it was a long search for just a pocketful of decent contenders.

But before we got to the conker trees the leaves would be so thick they would be up to our knees. You could bury yourself in those wonderful leaves. Swim even. Almost inevitably the leaf fight would start. Filling the hood of your opponent's duffel coat was a favourite tactic. I suspect the leaf fight was as important as the conkers on these woodland expeditions – a celebration of early winter made up of testosterone and a sense of freedom and that rich, deep, slightly fungal smell of new humus: the very stuff of which the soil and the Earth and childhood are made.

26 November 2012

CLAXTON

It was the first peregrine of the winter and although I couldn't initially see it, I knew it was among this maelstrom of birds that had been thrown up across the northern horizon. No other regularly occurring raptor has that kind of impact on my patch. It triggers a bow-wave of dread, which affects not only geese many times its own weight, but also birds as small as finches that would be mere morsels to the falcon.

A criss-cross pattern of several thousand pink-footed geese was spread skywards for more than a kilometre. Amid their glorious barking chorus were the more musical anxiety calls of Canada geese and the nails-on-blackboard braying of greylags. They descended then rose several times and on each occasion the waves of wildfowl refuelled a general panic. A tight thousand-strong press of golden plover roved through the others like a mobile storm, while above were thinly spread flights of lapwings, starlings, ruff and black-tailed godwits.

I'm always struck how this one apex predator even has its impact on many of the humans walking in this landscape. Birdwatchers were catching on to the wider mood and scanning the heavens in random sweeps. I too picked through as many of the flocks as possible, but still I couldn't find the one cruciform shape that was the source of the whole tableau.

There was an element of bathos in its final discovery. I eventually sifted the random motion down to an epicentre where a bolus of mixed birds was rising and dropping across the field in a sequence of wild wind-lifted bursts. Ducks, waders and rooks were flitting and twisting in indecision and there right in the middle of them was a male peregrine perched on a gate. His breast was sparkling even in the November grey and there was poise and angle in the way he leaned forward – yet, like a cold star in its own turning galaxy of light and darkness, he never moved once.

28 November 2011

CLAXTON

A short-eared owl, one of the many that has invaded the county this autumn, was quartering the fields with its characteristic flight action, which involves a scissoring quick uplift and then a slow downward press of all that long-winged softness. For once, however, the glorious bird was upstaged by the marsh it patrolled. By three o'clock, even with the sun's full flare, I noticed how tongues of white mist surfaced all along the southern edge, their topmost layers wispy and loose-feathered. Directly beneath the sun itself there was a slow-shoaling wave of silent peach invading the fields and at 3.20 p.m. the Holstein cattle were hock-deep in sheets of it. Even just fifteen minutes later they were no more than elemental shapes sinking fast into a vague blur.

As I reached the River Yare, mist had welled up the sides, drifted on to the water from both banks and then rolled downstream with the river's own flow. Over on the other side, above Buckenham Marshes, golden plover and fieldfares swelled up out of the white in nervous wheeling flocks and were then swallowed again by all its softness. Pheasant calls, raucous and convulsive, erupted briefly from within it, their dark sounds seemingly soothed by the landscape's slow inexorable dissolution. At 4 p.m. only the treetops stood proud of the murk and I was so smothered in blurry darkness there was nothing for it but to plod home.

Yet it was weird to discover, as I rose up off the marsh, that the last dregs of daylight had suddenly spilled back on to the path. The sky above was again Antarctic blue. I could hear moorhens, snipe, mallard and magpies settling in the dykes or among the trees – trees that were now clear silhouettes from trunk to topmost twig. This last leakage of the day made me realise that it had not really gone dark any earlier than usual: rather, the sea-flat world of the Yare had just turned prematurely white.

30 November 2009

CLAXTON

I was delighted this week to receive a truly extraordinary message from a neighbour that someone has seen 'the panther' again in our parish. It was mentioned rather nonchalantly, simply as a wildlife tip that someone might pass on so that I could perhaps keep watch for it during my walks. I learnt subsequently that the tradition of seeing large black cats is well established in our area. The records are never quite substantiated with incontrovertible proof, but the creature has cropped up over many years, moving randomly around the neighbourhood. No one ever stops to reflect on where it goes and what it eats in between its human encounters, but no matter.

The sightings of inexplicable, potentially dangerous predators remind me of the eighteenth- and nineteenth-century traditions of a large black ghost dog in East Anglia that terrorised the locals under the name Black Shuck. The one constant in the reports is not so much any physical characteristics of the creature itself, but the frisson of excitement aroused in the observers. Perhaps we should see Black Shuck and the Claxton panther alike as metaphors for the notion – and perhaps even an expression of hope – of some unfathomable and residual power inherent in our somewhat toothless landscape.

This morning I encountered a like power of my own. A singing mistle thrush, the first pre-Christmas singing mistle thrush I have ever heard, launched that exquisite, high, far-away song on to a cold-edged west wind. It brimmed up and filled the whole village with similar feelings of hope. Recall, perhaps, that this glorious motif has been passed on, thrush to thrush, since the retreat of the ice, when this forested edge of Europe became a place fit once more for missies. It is a song from long before the idea of England, older even than this island itself. Yet it wells up refreshed out of the soil every year. That truly seems cause for a sense of mystery.

DECEMBER

1 December 2008

Claxton

As I walked along the bank a male kestrel, facing down into the breeze, kept fractionally ahead of me. Its hovering just above eye level was not particularly noteworthy but its refusal to relinquish one spot of cold air over the dead vegetation did make me wonder. What could it see? Then it went down through the reeds. The acuity of its entry was like a paper knife between the flap and the envelope. Back up it came, as if the descent and rise were part of one sweet manoeuvre. For less than a second, perhaps, there was a slight laboriousness before departure. It was this that enabled me to pick out the pigeon's-egg-sized bulge in the talons. Yet the yellow-scaled feet were so tightly closed over the prey that one sensed the beat had already gone from a tiny heart.

A life had passed so casually. A kestrel had taken its prey and flown off, all in a matter of seconds. A sense of ordinariness was already reassembling itself within the landscape. As I committed it to my notebook, I could find no false sense of drama to inject into the scene. Yet in a forty-year career I'd never seen it before. I doubt I'll ever witness it again.

For, unmistakably, there it was, the pert upward jut of a wren's tail in those claws. I've trawled the literature. I can find no mention of a wren ever falling victim to a kestrel before. (Although there is a reference to an occupied wren's nest lodged in the fabric of a kestrel's own.) It seemed so improbable that I paced out over the marsh to the exact spot where the falcon had landed and was winnowing shreds of down from the body. I have them on my desk as I type these words – the telltale brown, barred flight feathers, so small that in full fan the wings would look nothing larger than a pair of earrings to adorn a pagan.

4 December 2006

WHEATACRE, NORFOLK

Beyond the A143 to Yarmouth is a spur of 'upland' (a relative term in our area since it is no more than twenty metres high) bounded to the south, north and east by a long snaking bend of the River Waveney. It is a peninsula with three tiny villages, no through road and very little traffic, which make for an immensely peaceful place.

My favourite stretch is Gunstead's Carr, the alder wood running along its northern edge. The rabbits have warrened the sandy substrate, reminding me that this was once an ancient beach, while the open grass flats beyond were an arm of the North Sea. Reclamation over two thousand years has converted it into terra firma, but I cannot help feeling that at Gunstead's any human visitor is on the edge of something.

The carr has a wonderful atmosphere. The sandy tree-covered slope runs down into a black, boggy sump at the marsh edge that has an almost tropical intimacy. Old coppiced alders, multi-stemmed and broad-topped, rise out of the wet mulch to dominate the canopy, but, at ground level, one is enmeshed in a hazel understorey. These bushes have ancient root stocks that mix new and old sprouts. The living tissue has retreated to the line of the fresh shoots but any exposed lengths beyond have withered to acquire the shattered, gnarled quality of a witch's nose or her arthritic hands.

The rich suggestive mixture of wooded shadow and black swamp is good for all sorts of birds and the farmer tells me that after clear moonlit nights Gunstead's is a great place for woodcock. But I had to make do with the woodcock owl – the short-eared owl – so named in Norfolk because the two migrant birds arrive on the same east wind. My bird hunted in broad daylight, its scissor wings snipping the winter air with elastic ease.

5 December 2005

CLAXTON

It was one of those mornings when the dim browns and greens of the winter landscape were blurred further by mist. They seemed to induce their internal corollary in a kind of mental fog. But in an instant it was blasted away when I noted flocks of waders and duck whose silhouetted flight-lines crazed the empty sky. Only one creature has that power over its fellow birds and I located the male peregrine as he sallied down four or five times in succession, each dive sending out a secondary bow-wave of anxiety.

Being a spectacle wearer I marvel at birds' acuity of vision. And here I mean not just that of the peregrine itself, whose eyes are larger than our own, but the birds put to flight. One of their number somehow always manages to spot the threatening speck in the sky and raise the alarm. In fact, it's an old birder's trick to respond to these movements of dread and find its origins.

All the writers captivated by the peregrine – who culminate in the figure of J. A. Baker, the author of *The Peregrine*, surely one of the finest works on nature in the English language – seem to be compelled to ever-higher superlatives in honouring this species. I think these responses have their origins in the bird's capacity to transform the mood of an entire landscape.

Think of it: one solitary two-pound creature whose anchor-like profile can trigger boiling clouds, sometimes involving tens of thousands of other birds. Imagine all their cumulative calories – many millions through one peregrine's entire lifetime – acquired laboriously from probing silt or dabbling aquatic vegetation, that are expended in that tumult of adrenalin and flight and speed. This morning a peregrine changed my day but I hope even more that, transmitted in mere shadow outline through these words, a peregrine's power may momentarily touch yours.

10 December 2012

CLAXTON

It was like a last cigarette butt swept up after the party – a bluebottle buzzing at the window, which initially got me to thinking about it. I tried to analyse it further as I took my walk across the marsh: what do I miss most in winter? Why should I feel a sense of absence? After all, many of the old favourites are in place regardless of the season. The blackbirds are on the lawn as the door closes and when I pass the last houses down the lane the starlings are still upon the pot tops to repeat their self-delighting inward rambling song.

Beyond the kissing gate no single tree has yet moved. They're all still here and, while they're now stripped bare of foliage, they will make that heroic outstretched stand winter-long. If anything the reeds are more beautiful during the dead time, their stems a rich cinnamon and their heads a sparkling floss in the sunlight. There is even a particular harvest that is lost once spring arrives. Today I can enjoy it all: the glorious canine music from the pink-footed geese and that special quietness of a stonechat on its fence top.

Yet what I miss most is the insects, those relatives of that bluebottle, whose warmth-loving soft-bodied forms are incinerated in the scorching colours of autumn. Winter is insect free and it makes you think about all their gifts through the year:

the shapeless clouds of chironomid midges choiring down the dyke at last light; the glancing maypole weave of butterflies and bumblebees around the flowering bramble; then all those sleeping beauties in my moth trap – maybe sixty to seventy species on a good summer's night – that always add a spoonful of excitement to moth day (Saturday mornings). Thank goodness for the December moth, an insect so subtly beautiful that it seems almost purpose-made to remind us of the aesthetic possibilities of chitin. What it also epitomises is the fugitive joys of insects. After all, no more than one in ten thousand of us has probably ever made the acquaintance of this routine garden familiar.

12 December 2011

CLAXTON

It was one of those strange days when the marsh blessed me with wonderful sightings, then seemed to take back even in the act of giving. First was a sparrowhawk, a female assailed by rooks as she dashed low along a dyke. Irritated by her tormentors, she suddenly left them all for dead with one of those sweet upward-surging curves that hawks delight in and which, on a graph, would have sent the whole boardroom into ecstasies. In seconds she'd vanished completely.

Next was a big female peregrine, heavily laden almost as if she were injured or, more likely, had a crop so bulging with meat she was struggling to fly. In truth I had seen far less of her than her consequences. Above the woods and fields were panicky spirals of rooks and golden plover, thrushes and duck all driving skywards and whenever she came closer to these potential prey, so the falcon triggered more intense but localised surges of terror. I followed this bow-wave until I finally spotted her, but she was so low to the field she seemed almost to have feet touched down. There was a dragging air to the flight, she slowed and faltered into a mound of vegetation never to rise again. I stood hoping and watching with binoculars until I could stand the fatiguing ache in my arms no more.

Worst and best of the day was the moment I rose up the river bank and there was an otter sailing calmly towards me through the wind-splintered blue sheen of the water. She chewed with relish on a last mouthful of fish and was swimming at a slight angle to my position. I had hopes when she surfaced next that I would have a perfect view. She never reappeared. Who knows how otters do it? They are masters of escapology. I scoured up and down the Yare for an hour. Strange to say, perhaps, I was not especially downhearted, just more determined to look again tomorrow.

14 December 2009

BURY ST EDMUNDS, SUFFOLK

When the half moon rose and dusk fell on the town's special Christmas market, nightfall seemed only to bring a deeper sense of intimacy and atmosphere to the heart of this delightful place. A drop in temperature also made the seasonal lights burn brighter. In one young Norwegian maple on a little street called The Traverse I noticed that its leafless branches were threaded with a circle of five twinkling white stars and eight other illuminations that attempted to mimic the momentary downward glow of a falling comet.

For once these adornments were outshone by an unscripted display laid on by the natural world. Judging from the wide sphere of white droppings that covered the litterbins and cycle lock-up rails below, I guess that this one urban tree has been used by pied wagtails as a roost throughout the winter. This was clearly their moment to assemble, the birds flitting nervously between its bare branches and the adjacent roof of Bury's Corn Exchange. Trafficking back and forth, they showered upon the neon-lit street a constant rainfall of *chizzick* and *swi-soo* contact notes. Like white flakes of sound these calls also drifted into the versions of 'Come Fly With Me' and Dave Brubeck's 'Take Five' that the live saxophonist performed from the adjacent building. It created an unrepeatable but wonderful soundscape that not even the boom bass of the boy racers could touch.

Pedestrians stopped to stare. One witness, cigarette in hand, sleeveless, white badger stripe through his aged punk's thatch, discussed them with his mates. Were they sparrows? one woman asked. It was a classic English street in winter made up of the utterly quotidian – the neon from the Café Rouge, the Norwich & Peterborough, the Britannia and the Abbey and a pub called the Nutshell, but the vision of those roosting wagtails, about five hundred of them, their tails all seeming to wag at once, elevated the moment to a condition of epiphany.

17 December 2007

CLAXTON

It was the wigeon that made me think. Hundreds of birds kept rising and wheeling away across the cloudless sky, then they would fly back to the open water, land and, for some unknown reason, rise again. The whole cycle of action resolved into just two basic sounds – the high, clear whistling that we can easily imitate but never capture in speech. The bird's old local names – whim, whewer, whew and smee – convey our attempts but little of the falling notes' alchemical powers. In concert wigeon calls are somehow the sounds of the cold and the ice blue and the huge empty spaces. If anything, the sounds of the air through their wings and that of their feet upon the water were more mysterious still. All of this kinetic energy was compressed by the distance and the inadequacy of human hearing to just one noise, which rather resembled a large boat cutting a heavy wake at intervals.

Once attuned, I realised that I was hearing only a fraction, or nothing whatsoever, of an entire landscape of activity. Seeing a feeding deer, I could gather neither the neat, sharp prick of its hoof into the grass nor the softness of breath across that broad dark muzzle. More frustrating was the way I could 'see' the sounds of a golden plover flock. About two hundred birds turned as one and you know that with each twist of those four hundred wings, the stream of air roaring above and below each one unleashes an accompanying whoosh of wind. I picked up little except, as consolation, the winding faience melody of their calls, like a briefly opened music box at the very edge of one's hearing. Furthest away of them all was the hunting barn owl. Its wings in the sunlight had a flickering silvery quality. It is often said that the owl's flight is completely silent yet, at some level, surely, all that moth's softness must have its own microscopic music.

18 December 2006

CLAXTON

Whenever I go down to the Yare, I always make for the same spot: the red-brick block that houses the only water pump on these levels and the one structure able to incise a small ellipse of shelter from the winds that have blasted the valley for days.

I luxuriated in its pocket of stillness, just as the rooks and jackdaws above me were exhilarated by the wind. They cruised overhead in long linear flocks, their calls ricocheting back through their numbers. At a point close to their roost, they swirled, riding the currents of air to a virtual standstill, before careering down to the fields in a helter-skelter rush. Before darkness all rose in a swarm to enter their roost, when I estimated about 25,000 birds.

For once this spectacle took second place to an unexpected diversion on the river bank. Two peregrines decided to spend their night in a tall willow close to where I stood. I'd picked out the first bird, a female, hurtling low over the river, lashing down on the wind with those meticulous, brutal wing strokes. In a second she had sallied through the trees and out over the marsh virtually upending a greylag goose in mid-flight, whose brash honking calls swelled up with hysteria.

The bigger bird crashed to the ground in terror, just as the peregrine rose and turned to make straight for the treetop close by. A smaller bird, a tiercel, joined her and through the wind I could hear their conversation, a high repeated call with a metallic, petulant edge.

As night fell they faded to shadows. I could sense the female swoop occasionally out over the river to reassure herself and then return, but the male doggedly clung to his swaying perch. I tried to imagine them in their little temporary domain: the peregrine heartbeats, the tautly strung calls and those eyes – eyes larger than a man's – opening and closing in the dark.

21 December 2001

CLAXTON

We think of them as the guardian spirits to our new home – two old female holly trees that flank the front gate and after which our house is named. They are much lopped and, while the bark holds a record of these wounds, the limbs have always been allowed to grow back, suggesting that our predecessors loved the sheltering greenery as much as we do now. After years of repeated pollarding the trees have developed into a wonderful upturned octopus of entangled branches, interlaced with wild clambering limbs of ivy. Hardly any light breaks through their canopy and it gives seclusion, even a hint of mystery, to one corner of the garden.

It is easy to see how the holly's 'darkly monumental foliage' – as Richard Mabey has memorably described it – maintains such a powerful grip on the European imagination. For centuries the species was used as a hedgerow or boundary tree, and an important part of its meaning in the landscape was a coded language of arbitrary division, ownership and power that only the human eye could decipher. Even now makers of British Ordnance Survey maps regard old holly trees as the best guide to the course of historic borders between parishes and neighbouring estates or farms.

In a pre-Christian era holly's affirmation of life in death gave it a religious significance. At the dead moment of the year the druids were said to deck their shrines with it as a symbol of rebirth, and during the Roman festival of Saturnalia, which was close in date to Christmas, people sent gifts to friends and family accompanied by sprays of holly.

Christians were unable to resist the pagan attachment to the tree and so simply entwined the evergreen foliage into their own rituals. Yet if one looks at the constituent parts of holly it seems designer-made as a Christian symbol. The red of the berries evokes the blood of Christ, the white flowers suggest his virgin birth and the prickly leaves his crown of thorns. Holly wood was eventually incorporated into the cross itself and holly saplings were said to have sprung up wherever Christ's feet touched the earth. Small wonder that we still deck our homes and churches with those indestructible dark leaves.

We had hoped to do the same at our house this Christmas, especially since both trees were initially smothered with a magnificent crop of crimson berries. But nature intended that our hollies would play a different kind of protective role. While the fruits have powerful emetic properties for humans, the birds love them and for the past few days a flock of redwings, migrant thrushes from Scandinavia, have moved into the garden and systematically stripped the trees bare. Only a few clusters remain on the most exposed branches while the ground beneath is bespattered with the indigestible remains of the fruit.

Yet these events have not been without their compensations. Redwings are intensely shy thrushes, so the near-darkness of the holly canopy was perfect camouflage for their theft. Every now and then one of them would loom into a shaft of sunshine to reveal the brilliant chestnut of its underwing and an intense white brow above a dark eye-line as bold as tiger stripes. Then it would melt back into the shadow, where the whole flock sustained a burbling sub-song as they feasted. What better message could one have for the revival of life in the coming new year?

22 December 2003

MINSMERE, SUFFOLK

It tipped down all day at this RSPB reserve and seemed to send the ducks into wild ecstasies. Flocks of teal flung themselves into the wind and downpour as they commuted across the marsh without any obvious motive other than the pleasures of rainfall.

A group of drake shovelers below the hide showed the same relish for the conditions. Several flew to join them and as they landed, the plasticine-orange feet, spread for the moment of impact, sent up a wake of spray before their owners belly-flopped in. They rode the cold grey slap of the pool like corks. Neither the rain nor the dull light could reduce their wonderful colours: the linen-white breasts, the emerald heads and oblongs of dusky chestnut on their sides. Every now and then when one of them rolled, a sheet of grey water would slide off the flanks like hot oil off Teflon. It would thrust its head under and one wondered what those yellow eyes could see in the muddy blur, then up it would come to reveal the bottle-green head shining like some finely polished stone. The only impact of the long dunk was a scattering of droplets on an instantly dry surface.

The waterproofing of a duck's plumage is a given but as I watched their antics I realised just how indifferent they were to the elements. They were in these miserable conditions but not at all oppressed. Thereafter I couldn't help seeing the shovelers, perhaps because of those luminous, manufactured colours, as supremely detached. Like a supermarket carrier-bag bellied out with wind but snagged in a winter hedge, they expressed the wider landscape but were somehow completely other than it.

24 December 2012

CHEE DALE, DERBYSHIRE

The most forbidding of the dales along the River Wye is a glorious landscape that entails hard-won negotiations between the limestone, the ash woods and ourselves. Through the crags and the brooding moss-smothered chaos of the trees, the Victorians inserted a slender thread of human order in the shape of the Midland Railway that opened in 1863. It is a mere ghost now. The trains, with all the forward momentum of those steam clouds and steel tracks, have gone, but the silent beds of clinker and the succession of dank tunnels under the cliffs still provide a perfectly clear run for walkers all the way to Bakewell.

It is at a point called the Rusher Cutting Tunnel that one can best appreciate the elements that comprise Chee Dale. Aside from the muted gush of the River Wye below, and the endless winter drip down the brick-lined mouth of the tunnel, the place is without sound. To the east the far slope is covered in ash and the distance underscores what contradictory trees they are. From afar the million pale twig ends across the canopy all somehow catch the light, giving to the whole mass a feathered or softly flossed quality.

Yet no single mature tree seems more mean-spirited than ash. The coppiced hazel already has catkins, there are quiet buds even now on blackthorn, while the solitary yews are an intense song of green on the crags opposite. But there are no such frivolities on ash. Their mere hue, a kind of bone white, speaks of niggardliness. In fact, if limestone itself could sprout leaves, it would take the form of this magnificent tree. And who does not admire its toughness? At one slope too steep for human footprint at least three hundred ash saplings have scrambled up to the soaring bluffs above, dragging an understorey of ivy and bramble with them, filling the thin seams of soil with life and, come summer, mothering it all in that fine-cut fretted shadow of fresh ash leaves.

27 December 2010

CLAXTON

I was taken completely by surprise as it surfaced in the dyke just next to where I was standing. Almost immediately I could tell it was an otter – a large dog otter, to be precise. He was swimming at the surface, his great square head resting on the shallow bow-wave that his progress pushed just ahead of him. The body fur of his curving back was slicked-down oily. The seal's whiskers were long and sparse and dangled to the waterline. In his wake and washing to the sides was a widening recessional of ripples, whose crests were picked out by weak moonlight, so that his passage had a gloriously glittering quality.

I was struck most by the tail as it trailed loosely behind the owner. It was vertically compressed so that it had some of the flattened character of a beaver's tail. He carried it just marginally above the water's surface, and every now and again he would arch and dive and that rudder would rise as a final curved flag of his going. I got into a rhythm of watching him for one or two dives and then, after the next, I'd run in parallel down the snow-covered track so that I could be much closer to the spot where he eventually reappeared.

His typical progress was to dive, surface, paddle a few seconds and dive again. But every now and then he would dive and barely surface before going instantly back under, showing himself merely as an expanding circle of ripples. I wondered if he had spotted something that required an immediate closer inspection. However, the ensuing return to the surface seemed to require some additional expression of an otter's supple powers. And up he came, dolphin-like, a third of the body rising clear of the tin-coloured water, like something made of cork and held down under pressure, then suddenly released. He did this at least four times before I finally lost him in the dark.

It struck me that there is a strange contradiction in the mechanical physics of otters. On the one hand it is the supreme swimmer among our terrestrial mammals and yet, despite this sub-aquatic prowess, no animal seems lighter, more buoyant and so full of air. It is as if the whole of an otter's body is filled with oxygen. Somehow one wouldn't be surprised if he suddenly took flight. And that, I suppose, is what they do, but underwater. Perhaps it is this seeming weightlessness that gives otters their additional aura of joy. For my second reflection on this snow-bound night was that even an otter's routine, eventless prosaic passage along a dyke expressed a kind of triumph. His mere presence filled even this death-girt landscape with life warmth that rippled outwards to me. And now, I hope, to you also.

28 December 2008

CLAXTON

Almost like a lover with a new flame I have made daily pilgrimage this month to a woodland in the parish that I'd never previously visited. It is a waterlogged alder carr flanked on one side by a raised bank and several fabulous large boundary oaks. But pride of place among the site's guardian trees is a huge octopus-like hawthorn. Seven coppiced limbs (one is smashed off by gales) fountain outwards in a gesture of silent, arthritic extravagance.

The heart of the wood is shin-deep in water and like all excessively damp environments it has that ambiguous air of decay and luxuriant growth. It is a place constructed of sunlight and trees and black soil, engineered by wind or fungus, then finished in thick green moss and ferns. The surface water must be very low in oxygen because many of the fallen leaves, which have sunk in deep layers to the bottom, are still perfectly green and intact. Through the clear water they quake as you walk like some eerily fluid mosaic.

Winter seems to be that much more strongly entrenched in this spot. Yet it has given me a generous sheaf of wildlife moments. Like the occasion I chanced on the smallest male sparrowhawk I've ever seen. Normally these wary birds flip away at your approach 'as quick as thought', as one author put it. But this one didn't even seem to see me. Perhaps he had just made an unsuccessful hunt and was momentarily exhausted. As he sat and simply watched I was able to take in the exact orange-tinged yellow of his irides.

Then there was the slender vixen who, in broad daylight, sauntered past me at just five metres' range. There is no English word for the economy of fox movements, even in such an off-beat, off-guard and relaxed mode. She sinewed through the trees and without pause, swallowed me down with her orange eye and passed on under the dark shadow.

I assumed she was looking for the same birds that I also search for daily. I love the teal, which cannon upwards in alarm, then return to scatter through the woods a thin, tiny, water-rinsed bell note like the tinkle of distant chimes. I hope even more to catch a glimpse of the woodcock. Mahogany brown, these waders often look black. As they uplift softly and twist away, there is sometimes a strange telltale sound, like the snapping taut of a small cotton sheet. That's normally all I experience. But it fills me with longing. Most intriguing of all is that in this cold, wet place, with all its moss-soft entanglements, where even I feel a deep relief on emerging into the fields of daylight, this bird passes the entire time, silent and secure.

28 December 2009

CLAXTON

As I left the house and tapped the bulb it read minus three degrees centigrade. The sky was a sheet of blue, the marsh a plane of white, and the air so dry and cold that my cheeks burned. It was not just the sight of a fox meandering over the field in broad daylight that suggested times were tough. As she ran, her thick brush curved windward from the line of her back. The crows rose one by one while she passed and landed just behind. All around from last night and the night before and the night before that were her zigzag tracks relentlessly driving everywhere – it was like that nightmare where the same thought recurs without end.

It felt as if the landscape had been stripped down and pushed right to the edge of hunger. Thrushes in the hedge picked at the last dried, dark berries. A pied wagtail walked on a puddle, slipping and faltering on the ice. Lapwings hunkered down so far into the snow that they were no more than dark blobs. The river, the only open water here for days, held about a thousand wigeon. They drifted away then sailed back in a tidal flotsam, whose motion was closely linked to my own passage along the bank. One sensed that their days of inactivity were a patient, brutal pitting of stored calories against time and the possibility of thaw.

As dusk fell, the creaking of the ice in the dykes and the snap sounds of broken reeds made it seem as if the whole place was being screwed down tighter still. The sun had gone, but a hemisphere of glorious apricot light sat as a capstone on the south horizon. Into this exquisite colour, with the physical impact of an otter into its pool, burst a peregrine. Then a second and (for me, without precedent in this valley) a third: a tiercel, fresh meat bulked at his crop, was perhaps an interloper into the territory of a pair.

The female of this couple and the unwanted male sparred so that he turned, claws uppermost to meet her feint. Her partner rose high above them both and then struck down. He pulled out of the dive long before impact, but all three were convulsed into loud calls. In almost all birds the source of avian sound, the syrinx, is far more sophisticated than the human voice box. But in the peregrine this muscle seems to have been pared down so that it yields a sound like a wire held under immense tension and struck with metal. The brutal clattering notes seemed both a shriek of pain and a voice of triumph. Then the three birds swerved away, I know not where, the darkness fell and I trudged home alone through the snow.

31 December 2007

CLAXTON

In the last days of the year I went to pay my respects to the oldest member of our village, a fine old hedgerow oak on the ancient track that leads to Ashby St Mary. It is not an especially tall tree, but it has a wonderfully grotesque elephantine boll that is about eight metres in circumference and is splashed liberally with a rich lichen green. An old formula for ageing trees – an inch (2.5 centemetres) of growth on the waistband each spring and summer – allows me to hazard a guess that this one is about 350 years old.

Despite my rather unflattering description of the oak, I find myself projecting on to it a decidedly feminine character. This arises from the striking asymmetry in the tree's profile, which involves an immense low bulge on one side. Yet her only trunk rises up from the opposite side and in combination they suggest a slender body emerging from one of those high-bustled Victorian dresses.

She long pre-dates, of course, the whole of the nineteenth century, and could easily have been a sapling as this nation briefly liberated itself from monarchy. When she was just the height of a man, the last wild wolves were being hounded out of Scotland, and less than a half-day's horse ride from where she stands there would still have been great bustards wandering the sandy flats of Breckland. Back then the men who worked the fields all around her would have earned the daily equivalent of a large loaf of bread and could have expected a hard-fought life of barely more than fifty years. Our oak, by contrast, has probably endured, cumulatively, that many years of solid rainfall, and more than an entire century of pure sunshine.

She is now the grand old dame of the village, a touchstone for all its occupants and an imaginative anchor with which to fix the memories of their ancestors throughout the modern era. She is also in a very real sense their living representative. As the writer Richard Mabey once put it so beautifully when we stood before her, she contains the exhaled carbon from the breath of everyone who has ever lived here.

She herself must have many offspring scattered locally, no doubt with acorn-burying jays and rooks acting as her many midwives. My recent visit was part of a plan to gather up a few more myself and then to ensure that she had even more local descendants. Alas, the mice, squirrels and birds had eaten them all over the autumn. I tried to bring within vision the vast time-lapse sequence showing the Noah's Ark of organisms that had fed from this oak over three and a half centuries. I now like to include my own family within that mental image, because, via the alchemy of words and print, the grand old dame has just put food on our table.

CLAXTON PARISH SPECIES LIST

Species lists and names are important not just to me personally but to all naturalists and, in fact, for all natural historical study. The former supply an enduring inventory, permitting us in minimal format to measure what and who lives in a particular location. Lists also allow us to see how an organism's residency might change over time. One list drawn up by my late neighbour Billy Driver in the 1960s and 1970s showed that tree sparrows once bred in Claxton (they are now almost extinct countywide). Another prepared by my seventeenth-century neighbour Sir Thomas Browne indicated that Eurasian Spoonbills once nested near our village (this bird only ended a 330-year breeding absence from this country in 1998).

Names are more important still. I am a passionate advocate of the need for English names for as many life forms as possible. Scientific Latin and Greek may be sufficient for specialists and may, on occasions, be the only way to refer to certain organisms. Wherever possible English equivalent names are a vital resource and aid.

They are in many ways the found poetry of natural science (Ghost Moth). They are variously freighted with humour (Common Stinkhorn or Long-winged Conehead), legend and folklore (Common Cuckoo), history (Pale-shouldered Brocade or Smoky Wainscot) and cultural texture (Primrose or Reed Canary Grass). They can evoke strange stories (Chicken of the Woods) and sometimes they inspire new stories (Horse-chestnut Leaf Miner). Each of them, however, is an open-ended proclamation about the possibility of a closer relationship. A name is an invitation to intimacy and even friendship.

Names are also powerfully political. An English name plants a flag for each species, giving it identity and accessibility, allowing human observers of all kinds to claim that living creature as part of their own experience.

Many wonderful animals are rendered beyond reach by complex scientific nomenclature. We need more anglicised names to allow everyone to share in a sense of connection and community. To give a single example, the hoverfly *Helophilus pendulus* is part of the very fabric of spring and summer for almost everyone in this country. It is the glorious saffron-striped insect that warms itself on sallow blossom in the first hot days of spring. It weaves endlessly through the buddleia cones in your summer garden. It dances down the bramble hedge in autumn, feasting on all that blue-black sweetness oozing out of the berries. It envelops the ivy flowers of October in its deliciously soft buzz. As you walk through the shaded wood edge it is the insect glinting in the one shaft of sunlight, flashing golden yellow before it vanishes like magic. You've seen it. It's your neighbour. Yet I suspect 99 per cent of us have no way to begin to shape and appreciate all these encounters, partly because until recently no common title for the insect existed. English names count.

I have tried to find anglicised names for as many as possible of the organisms I have encountered in my parish. I call *Helophilus pendulus* the Marsh Hoverfly, a name it has acquired in the last few years, although I can find no book using this anglicised version of the Latin *Helophilus* (literally 'marsh-loving'). Sometimes, in the absence of more guidance, I have simply made names up (e.g. White-banded Hoverfly for *Leucozona lucorum*).

The list has a number of features:

i. A species enclosed in square brackets refers to one assumed to have originated from captive stock (e.g. [Red-breasted Goose *Branta ruficollis*]).

ii. Occasionally a second name has been added but enclosed in ordinary brackets where the standardised international nomenclature differs from a more familiar British version (e.g. Tundra (Bewick's) Swan *Cygnus bewickii*).

iii. Sometimes alternative names have been given where two species are separable with great difficulty and usually only by microscopic examination (e.g. Yellow/Ophion Wasp *Ophion luteus/obscuratus*). I have preferred to list only what could be identified from photographic images or where dead specimens have been found. Occasionally after some names I add the abbreviation 'sp'. It indicates a species where there might be several extremely similar taxa (e.g. Water-crowfoot *Batrachium* sp).

iv. All the English names have initial capitals. Where no obvious common name exists I have listed a species with a title that reflects the type of organism to which it belongs. This is followed by its scientific name. These generic names are always in lower case (e.g. ground bug *Corizus hyoscyami*).

v. The names and taxonomic order for many groups have been taken or adapted from the following important titles:

Barnard, Peter *The Royal Entomological Society Book of British Insects*, Wiley-Blackwell, Oxford, 2011.

Beckett, Gillian, and Bull, Alec, *A Flora of Norfolk*, Norwich, 1999.

Brooks, Steve, and Lewington, Richard, *Field Guide to the Dragonflies and Damselflies of Great Britain and Ireland*, British Wildlife, Hook, 1997.

Chinery, Michael, *Insects of Britain and Western Europe*, A & C Black, London, 2007.

Evans, Martin and Edmonson, Roger, *A Photographic Guide to the Grasshoppers and Crickets of Britain and Ireland*, WGUK, 2007.

Gill, Frank and Donsker, David, (eds) *IOC World Bird List*, (v3.4). http://www.worldbirdnames.org [accessed 10/09/2013].
Stubbs, Alan and Falk, Steven, *British Hoverflies*, British Entomological Society and Natural History Society, Reading, 2002.
Thomas, Jeremy and Lewington, Richard, *The Butterflies of Britain and Ireland*, British Wildlife, Gillingham, 2010.

FUNGI
Velvet Shank *Flammulina velutipes*
Glistening Inkcap *Coprinus micaceus*
Oyster Mushroom *Pleurotus ostreatus*
Chicken of the Woods *Laetiporus sulphureus*
Blushing Bracket *Daedelopsis confragosa*
Soft Puffball *Lycoperdon molle*
Common Puffball *Lycoperdon perlatum*
Common Stinkhorn *Phallus impudicus*
Common Earthball *Scleroderma citrinum*
Jelly Ear *Auricularia auricula-judae*
Orange Peel Fungus *Aleuria aurantia*
Scarlet Elfcup *Sarcoscypha austriaca*

VASCULAR PLANTS
Water Horsetail *Equisetum fluviatile*
Field Horsetail *Equisetum arvense*
Marsh Horsetail *Equisetum palustre*
Bracken *Pteridium aquilinum*
Marsh Fern *Thelypteris palustris*
Male Fern *Dryopteris filix-mas*
Broad Buckler Fern *Dryopteris dilatata*
Scots Pine *Pinus sylvestris*
Corsican Pine *Pinus nigra*
White Water Lily *Nymphaea alba*
Yellow Water Lily *Nuphar lutea*
Rigid Hornwort *Ceratophyllum demersum*
Marsh Marigold *Caltha palustris*

Meadow Buttercup *Ranunculus acris*
Creeping Buttercup *Ranunculus repens*
Bulbous Buttercup *Ranunculus bulbosus*
Celery-leaved Buttercup *Ranunculus sceleratus*
Lesser Celandine *Ranunculus ficaria*
Greater Spearwort *Ranunculus lingua*
Lesser Spearwort *Ranunculus flammula*
Water-crowfoot *Batrachium* sp
Common Poppy *Papaver rhoeas*
Greater Celandine *Chelidonium majus*
Common Fumitory *Fumaria officinalis*
Wych Elm *Ulmus glabra*
Hop *Humulus lupulus*
Stinging Nettle *Urtica dioica*
Small Nettle *Urtica urens*
Beech *Fagus sylvatica*
Field Maple *Acer campestre*
Sycamore *Acer pseudoplatanus*
Horse Chestnut *Aesculus hippocastanum*
Pedunculate Oak *Quercus robur*
Silver Birch *Betula pendula*
Alder *Alnus glutinosa*
Hazel *Corylus avellana*
Good King Henry *Chenopodium bonus-henricus*
Fat-hen *Chenopodium album*
Spring Beauty *Montia perfoliata*
Thyme-leaved Sandwort *Arenaria serpyllifolia*
Common Chickweed *Stellaria media*
Greater Chickweed *Stellaria neglecta*
Greater Stitchwort *Stellaria holostea*
Marsh Stitchwort *Stellaria palustris*
Lesser Stitchwort *Stellaria graminea*
Bog Stitchwort *Stellaria alsine*
Common Mouse-ear *Cerastium holosteiodes*
Water Chickweed *Myosoton aquaticum*

Mossy Pearlwort *Sagina procumbens*
Ragged Robin *Lychnis flos-cuculi*
White Campion *Silene alba*
Red Campion *Silene dioica*
Amphibious Bistort *Polygonum amphibium*
Redshank *Polygonum persicaria*
Knotgrass *Polygonum aviculare*
Sheep's Sorrel *Rumex acetosella*
Common Sorrel *Rumex acetosa*
Broad-leaved Dock *Rumex obtusifolius*
Great Water Dock *Rumex hydrolapathum*
Marsh Dock *Rumex palustris*
Perforate St John's-wort *Hypericum perforatum*
Square-stalked St John's-wort *Hypericum tetrapterum*
Common Mallow *Malva sylvestris*
Common Dog-violet *Viola riviniana*
Field Pansy *Viola arvensis*
White Bryony *Bryonia dioica*
Aspen *Populus tremula*
Crack Willow *Salix fragilis*
White Willow *Salix alba*
Almond Willow *Salix triandra*
Goat Willow *Salix caprea*
Grey Willow *Salix cinerea*
Hedge Mustard *Sisymbrium officinale*
Garlic Mustard *Alliaria petiolata*
Thale-cress *Arabidopsis thaliana*
Common Winter-cress *Barbarea vulgaris*
Watercress *Rorippa nasturtium-aquaticum*
Lady's Smock *Cardamine pratensis*
Wavy Bitter-cress *Cardamine flexuosa*
Hairy Bitter-cress *Cardamine hirsuta*
Common Whitlow-grass *Erophila verna*
Shepherd's Purse *Capsella bursa-pastoris*
Swine-cress *Coronopus squamatus*

Wild Mignonette *Reseda lutea*
Primrose *Primula vulgaris*
Yellow Loosestrife *Lysimachia vulgaris*
Bog Pimpernel *Anagallis tenella*
Scarlet Pimpernel *Anagallis arvensis*
Red Currant *Ribes rubrum*
Meadowsweet *Filipendula ulmaria*
Bramble *Rubus fruticosa*
Raspberry *Rubus idaeus*
Silverweed *Potentilla anserina*
Tormentil *Potentilla erecta*
Wild Strawberry *Fragaria vesca*
Wood Avens *Geum urbanum*
Agrimony *Agrimonia eupatoria*
Dog Rose *Rosa canina*
Cherry plum *Prunus cerasifera*
Blackthorn *Prunus spinosa*
Crab Apple *Malus sylvestris*
Rowan *Sorbus aucuparia*
Hawthorn *Crataegus mongyna*
Greater Bird's-foot Trefoil *Lotus pedunculatus*
Tufted Vetch *Vicia cracca*
Common Vetch *Vicia sativa*
Meadow Vetchling *Lathyrus pratensis*
Black Medick *Medicago lupulina*
Red Clover *Trifolium pratense*
Gorse *Ulex europaeus*
Purple Loosestrife *Lythrum salicaria*
Great Willowherb *Epilobium hirsutum*
Marsh Willowherb *Epilobium palustre*
Rosebay Willowherb *Chamaenerion angustifolium*
Common Evening-primrose *Oenothera biennis*
Enchanter's Nightshade *Circaea lutetium*
Holly *Ilex aquifolium*
Sun Spurge *Euphorbia helioscopia*

Petty Spurge *Euphorbia peplus*
Meadow Cranesbill *Geranium pratense*
Herb Robert *Geranium robertianum*
Common Stork's-bill *Erodium cicutarium*
Common Ivy *Hedera helix*
Pennywort *Hyrocotyle vulgaris*
Sanicle *Sanicula europaea*
Rough Chervil *Chaerophyllum temulum*
Cow Parsley *Anthriscus sylvestris*
Alexanders *Smyrnium olustratum*
Ground Elder *Aegopodium podagraria*
Lesser Water-parsnip *Berula erecta*
Fennel *Foeniculum vulgare*
Hemlock *Conium maculatum*
Fool's Watercress *Apium nodiflorum*
Wild Angelica *Angelica sylvestris*
Upright Hedge Parsley *Torilis japonica*
Common Hogweed *Heracleum sphondylium*
Wild Carrot *Daucus carota*
Wild Privet *Ligustrum vulgare*
Black Nightshade *Solanum nigrum*
Bittersweet *Solanum dulcamara*
Field Bindweed *Convolvulus arvensis*
Hedge Bindweed *Calystegia sepium*
Bog-bean *Menyanthes trifoliata*
Green Alkanet *Pentaglottis sempervirens*
Water Forget-me-not *Myosotis scorpioides*
Tufted Forget-me-not *Myosotis laxa*
Field Forget-me-not *Myosotis arvensis*
Changing Forget-me-not *Myosotis discolor*
Hedge Woundwort *Stachys sylvatica*
White Dead Nettle *Lamium album*
Red Dead Nettle *Lamium purpureum*
Bugle *Ajuga reptans*
Ground Ivy *Glechoma hederacea*

Self-heal *Prunella vulgaris*
Marjoram *Origanum vulgare*
Gipsywort *Lycopus europaeus*
Water Mint *Mentha aquatica*
Common Water-starwort *Callitriche stagnalis*
Greater Plantain *Plantago major*
Ribwort Plantain *Plantago lanceolata*
Butterfly bush *Buddleja davidii*
Ash *Fraxinus excelsior*
Common Privet *Ligustrum vulgare*
Great Mullein *Verbascum thapsus*
Common Figwort *Scrophularia nodosa*
Common Toadflax *Linaria vulgaris*
Foxglove *Digitalis purpurea*
Germander Speedwell *Veronica chamaedrys*
Brooklime *Veronica beccabunga*
Wood Speedwell *Veronica montana*
Field Speedwell sp *Veronica polita/agrestis*
Common Butterwort *Pinguincula vulgaris*
Fen Bedstraw *Galium uliginosum*
Marsh Bedstraw *Galium palustre*
Cleavers *Galium aparine*
Elder *Sambucus nigra*
Honeysuckle *Lonicera periclymenum*
Moschatel *Adoxa moschatellina*
Marsh Valerian *Valeriana dioica*
Teasel *Dipsacus fullonum*
Devil's-bit Scabious *Succisa pratensis*
Greater Burdock *Arctium lappa*
Musk Thistle *Cirsium nutans*
Spear Thistle *Cirsium vulgare*
Marsh Thistle *Cirsium palustre*
Creeping Thistle *Cirsium arvense*
Cotton Thistle *Onopordum acanthium*
Common Knapweed *Centaurea nigra*

Nipplewort *Lapsana communis*
Bristly Oxtongue *Picris echioides*
Marsh Sow-thistle *Sonchus palustris*
Smooth Sow-thistle *Sonchus oleraceus*
Prickly Sow-thistle *Sonchus asper*
Dandelion *Taraxacum officinale*
Beaked Hawk's-beard *Crepis vesicaria*
Fox and Cubs *Pilosella aurantiaca*
Common Cudweed *Filago germanica*
Common Fleabane *Pulicaria dysenterica*
Common Daisy *Bellis perennis*
Feverfew *Tanacetum parthenium*
Tansy *Tanacetum vulgare*
Mugwort *Artemisia vulgaris*
Yarrow *Achillea millefolium*
Oxeye Daisy *Chrysanthemum leucanthemum*
Pineapple Weed *Matricaria discoidea*
Scentless Mayweed *Tripleurospermum inodorum*
Common Ragwort *Senecio jacobea*
Groundsel *Senecio vulgaris*
Colt's-foot *Tussilago farfara*
Hemp-agrimony *Eupatorium cannabinum*
Arrowhead *Sagittaria sagittifolia*
Water-plantain *Alisma plantago-aquatica*
Frogbit *Hydrocharis morsus-ranae*
Water Soldier *Stratiotes aloides*
Canadian Waterweed *Elodea canadensis*
Pondweed *Potamogeton compressus*
Lords and Ladies *Arum maculatum*
Greater Duckweed *Spirodela polyrhiza*
Common Duckweed *Lemna minor*
Ivy-leaved Duckweed *Lemna trisulca*
Least Duckweed *Lemna minuta*
Toad Rush *Juncus bufonius*
Blunt-flowered Rush *Juncus subnodulosus*

Jointed Rush *Juncus articulatus*
Sharp-flowered Rush *Juncus acutiflorus*
Hard Rush *Juncus inflexus*
Soft Rush *Juncus effusus*
Broad-leaved Cotton-grass *Eriophorum latifolium*
Common Spike-rush *Eleocharis palustris*
Black Bog Rush *Schoenus nigricans*
Greater Tussock Sedge *Carex paniculata*
Brown Sedge *Carex disticha*
Hairy Sedge *Carex hirta*
Lesser Pond Sedge *Carex acutiformis*
Greater Pond Sedge *Carex riparia*
Cypress Sedge *Carex pseudocyperus*
Bottle Sedge *Carex rostrata*
Carnation Sedge *Carex panicea*
Tawny Sedge *Carex hostiana*
Yellow Sedge *Carex viridula*
Common Sedge *Carex nigra*
Perennial Ryegrass *Lolium perenne*
Italian Ryegrass *Lolium multiflorum*
Crested Dog's-tail Grass *Cynosurus cristatus*
Quaking Grass *Briza media*
Annual Meadow Grass *Poa annua*
Cocksfoot Grass *Dactylis glomerata*
Reed Sweet Grass *Glyceria maxima*
Floating Sweet Grass *Glyceria fluitans*
False Oat Grass *Arrhenatherum elatius*
Yorkshire Fog *Holcus lanatus*
Sweet Vernal Grass *Anthoxanthum odoratum*
Reed Canary Grass *Phalaris arundinacea*
Common Bent *Agrostis capillaris*
Marsh Foxtail *Alopecurus geniculatus*
Black-grass *Alopecurus myosuroides*
Timothy *Phleum pratense*
Barren Brome *Bromus sterilis*

Common Couch-grass *Elytrigia repens*
Wall Barley *Hordeum murinum*
Common Reed *Phragmites australis*
Branched Bur-reed *Sparganium erectum*
Common Reedmace *Typha latifolia*
Lesser Reedmace *Typha angustifolia*
Bluebell *Hyacinthoides non-scripta*
Yellow Iris *Iris pseudocorus*
Black Bryony *Tamus communis*
Common Twayblade *Listera ovata*
Southern Marsh Orchid *Dactylorhiza praetermissa*
Early Marsh Orchid *Dactylorhiza incarnata*
Common Spotted Orchid *Dactylorhiza fuchsii*
Bee Orchid *Ophrys apifera*

BRYOPHYTES
Plagiomnium undulatum

LICHENS
Caloplaca flavescens
Diploica (Buellia) canescens

FLATWORMS PLATYHELMINES
CLASS TURBELLARIA
Polycelis nigra
Brandling Worm *Eisenia fetida*

SLUGS AND SNAILS
Garden Slug *Arion fuscus*
Large Black Slug *Arion ater*
Leopard Slug *Limax maximus*
Garden Snail *Helix aspersa*
Brown-lipped Snail *Cepaea nemoralis*
Copse Snail *Arianta arbustorum*

Common Amber Snail *Succinea putris*
Great Pond Snail *Lymnaea stagnalis*
Wandering Pond Snail *Lymnaea peregra*
Common Bithynia *Bithynia tentaculata*
The Ramshorn *Planorbis planorbis*
Mosculum lacustre

MILLIPEDES
Pill Millipede *Glomeris marginata*
Wood Louse *Philoscia muscorum*

SPIDERS AND RELATIVES
Lace weaver Spider *Amaurobius similis*
Daddy Long-legs Spider *Pholcus phalangoides*
Ground spider *Drassodes cupreus*
Crab Spider *Xysticus cristatus*
Zebra Spider *Salticus scenicus*
Spotted Wolf-spider/wolf-spider *Pardosa amentata /Pardosa prativaga*
Common Fox-spider *Alopecosa pulvurenta*
Rustic Wolf-spider *Trochosa ruricola*
Nursery Web Spider *Pisaura mirabilis*
Giant House Spider *Tegenaria duellica*
Funnel-web Spider *Agelena labyrinthica*
Cobweb Spider *Steatoda bipunctata*
Cobweb Spider *Anelosimus vittatus*
Comb-footed Spider *Enoplognatha ovata*
Long-jawed Orb-weaver Spider *Tetragnatha extensa*
Orb Stretch Spider *Meta segmentata/mengei*
Cave Spider *Meta merianae*
Garden Cross Spider *Araneus diadematus*
4-spot Orb-web Spider *Araneus quadratus*
Marbled Orb-web Spider *Araneus marmoreus*
Walnut Orb-web Spider *Nuctenea umbratica*

Furrow Spider *Larinioides cornutus*
Cucumber Green Spider *Araniella cucurbitina*
Common Hammock Weaver *Linyphia triangularis*
Harvestman *Phalangium opilio*
False-scorpion *Neobisium carcinoides*

INSECTS
DRAGONFLIES
Banded Demoiselle *Calopteryx splendens*
Emerald Damsel *Lestes sponsa*
Large Red Damselfly *Pyrrhosoma nymphula*
Azure Damselfly *Coenagrion puella*
Common Blue Damsel *Enallagma cyathigerum*
Blue-tailed Damsel *Ischnura elegans*
Red-eyed Damsel *Erythromma najas*
Hairy Dragonfly *Brachytron pratense*
Migrant Hawker *Aeshna mixta*
Southern Hawker *Aeshna cyanea*
Brown Hawker *Aeshna grandis*
Norfolk Hawker *Aeshna isosceles*
Emperor Dragonfly *Anax imperator*
Four-spotted Chaser *Libellula quadrimaculata*
Scarce Chaser *Libellula fulva*
Broad-bodied Chaser *Libellula depressa*
Black-tailed Skimmer *Orthetrum cancellatum*
Common Darter *Sympetrum striolatum*
Ruddy Darter *Sympetrum sanguineum*

GRASSHOPPERS AND CRICKETS
Oak Bush Cricket *Meconema thalassinum*
Dark Bush Cricket *Pholidoptera griseoaptera*
Roesel's Bush Cricket *Metrioptera roeselii*
Long-winged Conehead *Conocephalus discolor*
Short-winged Conehead *Conocephalus dorsalis*
Speckled Bush Cricket *Leptophyes punctatissima*

Common Green Grasshopper *Omocestus viridulus*
Field Grasshopper *Chorthippus brunneus*
Meadow Grasshopper *Chorthippus parallelus*
Lesser Marsh Grashopper *Chorthippus albomarginatus*
Common Earwig *Forficula auricularia*

BUGS AND RELATIVES
Hawthorn Shield Bug *Acanthosoma haemorrhoidale*
Parent Bug *Elasmucha grisea*
Green Shield Bug *Palomena prasina*
Sloe Shield Bug *Dolycoris baccarum*
Gorse Shield Bug *Piezodorus lituratus*
Forest Bug *Pentatoma rufipes*
Bronze Shield Bug *Troilus luridus*
Dock Shield Bug *Coreus marginatus*
Rhombic Leather Shield Bug *Syromastes rhombeus*
Tree Damsel Bug *Himacerus apterus*
Ground Bug *Corizus hyoscyami*
Ground Bug *Lygaeus saxatilis*
Mirid Bug *Deraeocoris ruber*
Mirid Bug *Liocoris tripustulatus*
Common Green Capsid *Lygocoris pabulinus*
Mirid Bug *Miris striatus*
Two-spotted Grass Bug *Stenotus binotatus*
Capsid Bug *Heterotoma planicornis*
Mirid Bug *Oncotylus viridiflavus*
Meadow Plant Bug *Leptoterna dolabrata*
Tarnished Plant Bug *Lygus rugulipennis*
Plant Bug *Notostira elongata*
Mirid Bug *Cyllecoris histrionius*
Common Pond Skater *Gerris lacustris*
Common Backswimmer *Notonecta glauca*
Common Froghopper *Philaenus spumarius*
Red-and-black Froghopper *Cercopis vulnerata*
Green Leafhopper *Cicadella viridis*

Aphid *Aphis* sp
Thrip *Thysanoptera* sp
Green Lacewing *Chrysoperla carnea*
scorpionfly *Panorpa* sp

BUTTERFLIES AND MOTHS
Small Skipper *Thymelicus sylvestris*
Essex Skipper *Thymelicus lineola*
Large Skipper *Ochlodes sylvanus*
Swallowtail *Papilio machaon*
Brimstone *Gonepteryx rhamni*
Large White *Pieris brassicae*
Small White *Pieris rapae*
Green-veined White *Pieris napi*
Orange-tip *Anthocharis cardamines*
Green Hairstreak *Callophrys rubi*
Purple Hairstreak *Neozephyrus quercus*
Small Copper *Lycaena phlaeas*
Brown Argus *Aricia agestis*
Common Blue *Polyommatus icarus*
Holly Blue *Celastrina argiolus*
White Admiral *Limenitis camilla*
Red Admiral *Vanessa atalanta*
Painted Lady *Vanessa cardui*
Small Tortoiseshell *Aglais urticae*
Peacock *Inachis io*
Comma *Polygonia c-album*
Speckled Wood *Pararge aegeria*
Meadow Brown *Maniola jurtina*
Wall *Lasiommata megera*
Ringlet *Aphantopus hyperantus*
Gatekeeper *Pyronia tithonus*

Ghost Moth *Hepialus humuli*
Orange Swift *Hepialus sylvina*

Common Swift *Hepialus lupulinus*
Six-spot Burnet *Zygaena filipendulae*
Hornet Clearwing *Sesia apiformis*
Red-tipped Clearwing *Synanthedon formicaeformis*
December Moth *Poecilocampa populi*
Oak Eggar *Lasiocampa quercus*
Emperor Moth *Saturnia pavonia*
Drinker *Euthrix potatoria*
Oak Hook-tip *Watsonalla binaria*
Pebble Hook-tip *Drepana falcataria*
Chinese Character *Cilix glaucata*
Peach Blossom *Thyatira batis*
Buff Arches *Habrosyne pyritoides*
Figure of Eighty *Tethea ocularis*
March Moth *Alsophila aescularia*
Large Emerald *Geometra papilionaria*
Common Emerald *Hemithea aestivaria*
Maiden's Blush *Cyclophora punctaria*
Clay Triple-lines *Cyclophora linearia*
Blood-vein *Timandra comae*
Small Blood-vein *Scopula imitaria*
Least Carpet *Idaea rusticata*
Small Fan-footed Wave *Idaea biselata*
Dwarf Cream Wave *Idaea fuscovenosa*
Small Dusty Wave *Idaea seriata*
Single-dotted Wave *Idaea dimidiata*
Treble Brown Spot *Idaea trigeminata*
Riband Wave *Idaea aversata*
Flame Carpet *Xanthorhoe designata*
Red Twin-spot Carpet *Xanthorhoe spadicearia*
Large Twin-spot Carpet *Xanthorhoe quadrifasiata*
Silver-ground Carpet *Xanthorhoe montanata*
Garden Carpet *Xanthorhoe fluctuata*
Common Carpet *Epirrhoe alternata*
Yellow Shell *Camptogramma bilineata*

Mallow *Larentia clavaria*
Purple Bar *Cosmorhoe ocellata*
Spinach *Eulithis mellinata*
Barred Straw *Eulithis pyraliata*
Small Phoenix *Ecliptopera silaceata*
Common Marbled Carpet *Chloroclysta truncata*
Barred Yellow *Cidaria fulvata*
Grey Pine Carpet *Thera obeliscata*
Spruce Carpet *Thera britannica*
Broken-barred Carpet *Electrophaes corylata*
Green Carpet *Colotygia pectinataria*
May Highflyer *Hydriomena impluviata*
Small Waved Umber *Horisme vitalbata*
White-banded Carpet *Spargania luctuata*
Scallop Shell *Rheumaptera undulata*
November Moth *Epirrita dilutata*
Winter Moth *Operophtera brumata*
Small Rivulet *Perizoma alchemillata*
Sandy Carpet *Perizoma flavofasciata*
Foxglove Pug *Eupithecia pulchellata*
Mottled Pug *Eupithecia exiguata*
Lime-speck Pug *Eupithecia centaureata*
Currant Pug *Eupithecia assimilata*
Tawny-speckled Pug *Eupithecia icterata*
Bordered Pug *Eupithecia succenturiata*
Larch Pug *Eupithecia lariciata*
V-Pug *Chloroclystis v-ata*
Green Pug *Pasiphila rectangulata*
Double-striped Pug *Gymnoscelis rufifasciata*
Treble-bar *Aplocera plagiata*
Small Yellow Wave *Hydrelia flammeolaria*
Yellow-barred Brindle *Acasis viretata*
Clouded Border *Lomaspilis marginata*
Seraphim *Lobophora halterata*
Scorched Carpet *Ligdia adustata*

Scorched Wing *Plagodis dolobraria*
Brimstone Moth *Opisthograptis luteolata*
Bordered Beauty *Epione repandaria*
Lilac Beauty *Apeira syringaria*
August Thorn *Ennomos autumnaria*
Canary-shouldered Thorn *Ennomos alniaria*
Dusky Thorn *Ennomos fuscantaria*
Early Thorn *Selenia dentaria*
Purple Thorn *Selenia tetralunaria*
Scalloped Hazel *Odontopera bidentata*
Scalloped Oak *Crocallis elinguaria*
Swallow-tailed Moth *Ourapteryx sambucaria*
Feathered Thorn *Colotois pennaria*
Brindled Beauty *Lycia hirtaria*
Oak Beauty *Biston strataria*
Peppered Moth *Biston betularia*
Mottled Umber *Erannis defoliaria*
Waved Umber *Menophra abruptaria*
Willow Beauty *Peribatodes rhomboidaria*
Mottled Beauty *Alcis repandata*
Pale Oak Beauty *Hypomecis punctinalis*
Engrailed *Ectropis bistortata*
Common White Wave *Cabera pusaria*
Common Wave *Cabera exanthemata*
Light Emerald *Campaea margaritata*
Pine Hawkmoth *Hyloicus pinastri*
Privet Hawkmoth *Sphinx ligustri*
Lime Hawkmoth *Mimas tiliae*
Eyed Hawkmoth *Smerinthus ocellata*
Poplar Hawkmoth *Laothoe populi*
Hummmingbird Hawkmoth *Macroglossum stellatarum*
Elephant Hawkmoth *Deilephila elpenor*
Puss Moth *Cerura vinula*
Sallow Kitten *Furcula furcula*
Iron Prominent *Notodonta dromedarius*

Pebble Prominent *Notodonta ziczac*
Lesser Swallow Prominent *Pheosia gnoma*
Swallow Prominent *Pheosia tremula*
Coxcomb Prominent *Ptilodon capucina*
Pale Prominent *Pterostoma palpina*
Marbled Brown *Drymonia dodonaea*
Lunar Marbled Brown *Drymonia ruficornis*
Chocolate-tip *Clostera curtula*
Buff-tip *Phalera bucephala*
Lobster Moth *Stauropus fagi*
Pale Tussock *Caliteara pudibunda*
Brown-tail *Euproctis chrysorrhoea*
Yellow-tail *Euproctis similis*
White Satin Moth *Leucoma salicis*
Black Arches *Lymantria monacha*
Rosy Footman *Miltochrista miniata*
Orange Footman *Eilema sororcula*
Dingy Footman *Eilema griseola*
Buff Footman *Eilema depressa*
Common Footman *Eilema lurideola*
Garden Tiger *Arctia caja*
White Ermine *Spilosoma lubricipeda*
Buff Ermine *Spilosoma luteum*
Muslin Moth *Diaphora mendica*
Ruby Tiger *Phragmatobia fuliginosa*
Cinnabar *Tyria jacobaeae*
Short-cloaked Moth *Nola cucullatella*
Least Black Arches *Nola confusalis*
Garden Dart *Euxoa nigricans*
Turnip Moth *Agrotis segetum*
Heart and Club *Agrotis clavis*
Heart and Dart *Agrotis exclamationis*
Dark Sword-grass *Agrotis ipsilon*
Shuttle-shaped Dart *Agrotis puta*
The Flame *Axylia putris*

Flame Shoulder *Ochropleura plecta*
Large Yellow Underwing *Noctua pronuba*
Lesser Yellow Underwing *Noctua comes*
Broad-bordered Yellow Underwing *Noctua fimbriata*
Lesser Broad-bordered Yellow Underwing *Noctua janthe*
Least Yellow Underwing *Noctua interjecta*
Ingrailed Clay *Diarsia mendica*
Small Square-spot *Diarsia rubi*
Setaceous Hebrew Character *Xestia c-nigrum*
Triple-spotted Clay *Xestia ditrapezium*
Double Square-spot *Xestia triangulum*
Six Striped Rustic *Xestia sexstrigata*
Square-spot Rustic *Xestia xanthographa*
Green Arches *Anaplectoides prasina*
Nutmeg *Discestra trifolii*
Cabbage Moth *Mamestra brassicae*
Dot Moth *Melanchra persicariae*
Pale-shouldered Brocade *Lacanobia thalassina*
Bright-line Brown Eye *Lacanobia oleracea*
Campion *Hadena rivularis*
Tawny Shears *Hadena perplexa*
Varied Coronet *Hadena compta*
Lychnis *Hadena bicruris*
Antler Moth *Cerapteryx graminis*
Hedge Rustic *Tholera cespitis*
Small Quaker *Orthosia cruda*
Powdered Quaker *Orthosia gracilis*
Common Quaker *Orthosia cerasi*
Clouded Drab *Orthosia incerta*
Twin-spotted Quaker *Orthosia munda*
Hebrew Character *Orthosia gothica*
Brown-line Bright-eye *Mythimna conigera*
Clay *Mythimna ferrago*
White-point *Mythimna albipuncta*
Striped Wainscot *Mythimna pudorina*

Common Wainscot *Mythimna pallens*
Shoulder-striped Wainscot *Mythimna comma*
Shark *Cucullia umbratica*
Mullein *Shargacucullia verbasci*
Pale Pinion *Lithophane hepatica*
Grey Shoulder-knot *Lithophane lactipennis*
Blair's Shoulder-knot *Lithophane leautieri*
Early Grey *Xylocampa areola*
Green-brindled Crescent *Allophyes oxyacanthae*
Merveille du Jour *Dichonia aprilina*
Brindled Green *Dryobotodes eremita*
Chestnut/Dark Chestnut *Conistra vaccinii/ligula*
Red-line Quaker *Agrochola lota*
Brown-spot Pinion *Agrochola litura*
Beaded Chestnut *Agrochola lychnidis*
Centre-barred Sallow *Atethmia centrago*
Lunar Underwing *Omphaloscelis lunosa*
Barred Sallow *Xanthia aurago*
Pink-barred Sallow *Xanthia togata*
Sallow *Xanthia icteritia*
Poplar Grey *Acronicta megacephala*
Sycamore *Acronicta aceris*
Alder Moth *Acronicta alni*
Dark Dagger/Grey Dagger *Acronicta tridens/psi*
Knot Grass *Acronicta rumicis*
Marbled Beauty *Cryphia domestica*
Copper Underwing/Svensson's Copper Underwing *Amphipyra pyramidea/berbera*
Mouse Moth *Amphipyra tragopoginis*
Old Lady *Mormo maura*
Bird's Wing *Dypterygia scabriuscula*
Brown Rustic *Rusina ferruginea*
Straw Underwing *Thalpophila matura*
Small Angle Shades *Euplexia lucipara*
Angle Shades *Phlogophora meticulosa*

Olive *Ipimorpha subtusa*
Suspected *Parastichtis suspecta*
Dingy Shears *Parastichtis ypsillon*
Dun-bar *Cosmia trapezina*
Dark Arches *Apamea monoglypha*
Light Arches *Apamea lithoxylaea*
Clouded-bordered Brindle *Apamea crenata*
Small Clouded Brindle *Apamea unanimis*
Rustic Shoulder-knot *Apamea sordens*
Double Lobed *Apamea ophiogramma*
Marbled Minor *Oligia strigilis*
Rufous Minor *Oligia versicolor*
Tawny Marbled Minor *Oligia latruncula*
Middle-barred Minor *Oligia fasciuncula*
Cloaked Minor *Mesoligia furuncula*
Common Rustic *Mesapamea secalis*
Lesser Common Rustic *Mesapamea didyma*
Small Wainscot *Chortodes pygmina*
Dusky Sallow *Eremobia ochroleuca*
Flounced Rustic *Luperina testacea*
Ear Moth *Amphipoea oculea*
Rosy Rustic *Hydraecia micacea*
Frosted Orange *Gortyna flavago*
Crescent *Celaena leucostigma*
Bulrush Wainscot *Nonagria typhae*
Twin-spotted Wainscot *Archanara geminipuncta*
Webb's Wainscot *Archanara sparganii*
Large Wainscot *Rhizedra lutosa*
Fen Wainscot *Arenostola phragmitidis*
Treble Lines *Charancya trigrammica*
Uncertain *Hoplodrina alsines*
Rustic *Hoplodrina blanda*
Vine's Rustic *Hoplodrina ambigua*
Mottled Rustic *Caradrina morpheus*
Pale Mottled Willow *Paradrina clavipalpis*

Cream-bordered Green Pea *Earias clorana*
Oak Nycteoline *Nycteola revayana*
Burnished Brass *Diachrysia chrysitis*
Goldspot *Plusia festucae*
Silver Y *Autographa gamma*
Beautiful Golden Y *Autographa pulchrina*
Plain Golden Y *Autographa jota*
Dark Spectacle *Abrostola triplasia*
Spectacle *Abrostola tripartita*
Red Underwing *Catocala nupta*
Blackneck *Lygephila pastinum*
Herald *Scoliopteryx libatrix*
Beautiful Hooktip *Laspeyria flexula*
Straw Dot *Rivula sericealis*
Snout *Hypena proboscidalis*
Fan-foot *Zanclognatha tarsipennalis*

MICRO-MOTHS
Plain Gold *Micropetrix calthella*
Horehound Longhorn *Nemophora fasciella*
Yellow-barred Longhorn *Nemophora degeerella*
Green Longhorn *Adela reaumurella*
Feathered Bright *Incurvaria masculella*
White-triangle Slender *Caloptilia stigmatella*
Horse-chestnut Leaf Miner *Cameraria ohridella*
Bird-cherry Ermine *Yponomeuta evonymella*
Willow Ermine *Yponomeuta rorrella*
Golden Argent *Argyresthia goedartella*
Diamond-back moth *Plutella xylostella*
Honeysuckle Moth *Ypsolopha dentella*
Four-spotted Obscure *Oegoconia quadripuncta*
Dingy Dowd *Blastobasis adustella*
London Dowd *Blastobasis lacticolella*
White-shouldered House Moth *Endrosis sarcitrella*
Brown House Moth *Hofmannophila pseudospretella*

Tinted Tubic *Crassa unitella*
Common Tubic *Alabonia geoffrella*
Sloe Flat-body *Loquetia lobella*
Brown-spot Flat-body *Agonopterix alstromeriana*
Brindled Flat-body *Agonopterix arenella*
Red-letter Flat-body *Agonopterix astromariana*
Poplar Comet *Batrachedra praeangusta*
White-legged Case-bearer *Coleophora albitarsella*
Buff Cosmet *Mompha ochraceella*
Dark Groundling *Bryotropha affinis*
Twenty-plume Moth *Alucita hexadactyla*
White Plume Moth *Pterophorus pentadactyla*
Beautiful Plume *Ambylyptilia acanthadactyla*
Common Plume *Emmelina monodactyla*
Hook-marked Straw Moth *Agapeta hamana*
Thistle Conch *Aethes cnicana*
Burdock Conch *Aethes rubigana*
Hemlock Yellow Conch *Aethes beatricella*
Black-headed Conch *Cochylis atricapitana*
Yellow Oak Button *Aleimma loeflingiana*
Maple Button *Acleris forsskaleana*
White-triangle Button *Acleris holmiana*
Garden Rose Tortrix *Acleris variegana*
Sallow Button *Acleris hastiana*
Grey Tortrix *Cnephasia* sp
Large Fruit-tree Tortrix *Archips podana*
Barred Fruit-tree Tortrix *Pandemis cerasana*
Cyclamen Tortrix *Clepsis spectrana*
Willow Marble *Apotomis lineana*
Plum Tortrix *Heyda pruniana*
Common Marble *Celypha lacunana*
Small Birch Bell *Epinotia ramella*
White-foot Bell *Epiblema foenella*
Bramble Shoot Moth *Notocelia uddmanniana*
Orange-spot Piercer *Pammene aurana*

Bee Moth *Aphomia sociella*
Large Tabby *Aglossa pinguinalis*
Rosy Tabby *Endotricha flammealis*
Gold Triangle *Hypsopygia costalis*
Double-striped Tabby *Hypsopygia glaucinalis*
Thicket Knot-horn *Acrobasis suavella*
Grey Knot-horn *Acrobasis advenella*
Ash-bark Knot-horn *Euzophora pinguis*
Garden Grass-veneer *Chrysoteuchia culmella*
Grass-veneer *Crambus pascuella*
Yellow Satin Veneer *Crambus perlella*
Pale-streak Grass-veneer *Agriphila selasella*
Common Grass-veneer *Agriphila tristella*
Elbow-stripe Grass-veneer *Agriphila geniculea*
Chequered Grass-veneer *Catoptria falsella*
Hook-tipped Grass-veneer *Platytes alpinilla*
Pale Water-veneer *Donacaula forficella*
Scarce Water-veneer *Donacaula mucronella*
Brown China-mark *Elophila nymphaeata*
Small China-mark *Cataclysta lemnata*
Ringed China-mark *Paraponyx stratiotata*
Beautiful China-mark *Nymphula stagnata*
Garden Pebble *Evergestis forficalis*
Small Purple and Gold *Pyrausta aurata*
European Corn Borer *Ostrinia nubilalis*
Small Magpie *Anania hortulata*
Elder Pearl *Anania coronata*
Olive Pearl *Udea olivalis*
Mother of Pearl *Pleuroptya ruralis*
Rush Veneer *Nomophila noctuella*

BEETLES
Ground Beetle *Carabus nemoralis*
Ground Beetle, *Elaphrus cupreus*
Burying Beetle *Nicrophorus investigator*

Burying Beetle *Necrodes littoralis*
Burying Beetle *Oiceoptoma thoracicum*
Devil's Coach Horse *Ocypus olens*
Darkling Beetle *Diaperis boleti*
Dung Beetle *Aphodius rufipes*
Lesser Stag Beetle *Dorcus parallelipipedus*
Common Cockchafer *Melolontha melolontha*
Summer Chafer *Amphimallon solstitiale*
Bloodsucker *Rhagonycha fulva*
Click Beetle *Ampedus sanguineolentus*
Chequered Click Beetle *Prosternon tessellatum*
Click Beetle *Athous haemorrhoidalis*
Willow Flea Beetle *Crepidodera aurata*
Pollen Beetle *Meligethes aeneus*
Garden Sap Beetle *Glischrochilus hortensis*
Soldier Beetle *Cantharis rustica*
Common Cardinal Beetle *Pyrochroa serraticornis*
Spotted Longhorn Beetle *Rutpela maculata*
Wasp Longhorn Beetle *Clytus arietis*
Lesser Thorn-tipped Longhorn Beetle *Pogonocherus hispidus*
Red Longhorn Beetle *Stictoleptura rubra*
Malachite Beetle *Malachius bipustulatus*
Reed Leaf Beetle *Donacia vulgaris*
False Ladybird *Endomychus coccineus*
2-spot Ladybird *Adalia bipunctata*
7-spot Ladybird *Coccinella 7-punctata*
22-spot Ladybird *Psyllobora 22-punctata*
10-Spot Ladybird *Adalia 10-punctata*
Harlequin Ladybird *Harmonia axyridis*
14-spot Ladybird, *Propylea 14-punctata*
Cream-spot Ladybird *Calvia 14-guttata*
18-spot Ladybird *Myrrha octodecimguttata*
Varied Carpet Beetle *Anthrenus verbasci*
Rosemary Beetle *Chrysolina americana*
Green Tortoise Beetle *Cassida viridis*

Thick-legged Flower Beetle *Oedemera nobilis*
Yellow Mealworm Beetle *Tenebrio molitor*
Black Vine Weevil *Otiorhynchus sulcatus*
Nettle Weevil *Phyllobius pomaceus*
Pea-leaf Weevil *Sitona lineatus*
Figwort Weevil *Cionus scrophulariae*
Great Silver Beetle *Hydophilus piceus*
Whirligig Beetle *Gyrinus natator*

FLIES
Large Bee-fly *Bombylius major*
Yellow Swarming-fly *Thaumatomyia notata*
Hoverfly *Melanostoma mellinum*
Hoverfly *Melanostoma scalare*
Hoverfly *Epistrophe eligans*
Marmalade Hoverfly *Episyrphus balteatus*
Hoverfly *Eupeodes luniger*
White-banded Hoverfly *Leucozona lucorum*
Hoverfly *Melangyna umbellatarum/labiatarum*
Hoverfly *Scaeva pyrastri*
Hoverfly *Sphaerophoria scripta*
Common Banded Hoverfly *Syrphus ribesii*
Hoverfly *Syrphus vitripennis*
Hoverfly *Xanthogramma pedissequum*
Hoverfly *Chrysotoxum bicinctum*
Hoverfly *Cheilosia variabilis*
Hoverfly *Ferdinandea cuprea*
Heineken Hoverfly *Rhingia campestris*
Hoverfly *Lejogaster metallina*
Hoverfly *Eristalinus sepulchralis*
Bright Dronefly *Eristalis horticola*
Furry Dronefly *Eristalis intricarius*
Common Dronefly *Eristalis tenax*
Tapered Dronefly *Eristalis pertinax*
Marsh Hoverfly *Helophilus pendulus*

Yellow-faced Hoverfly *Helophilus trivittatus*
Dead-Head Hoverfly *Myathropa florea*
Narcissus Bulb Fly *Merodon equestris*
Hoverfly *Pipiza noctituca*
Bog Hoverfly *Sericomyia silentis*
Bumblebee Hoverfly *Volucella bombylans*
Inane Hoverfly *Volucella inanis*
Pellucid Hoverfly *Volucella pellucens*
Thick-legged Hoverfly *Syritta pipiens*
Hoverfly *Xylota segnis*
Thick-headed Fly *Sicus ferrugineus*
Ensign Fly *Sepsis fulgens*
Fruit Fly *Platyparea discoidea*
Fruit Fly *Oxyna parietina*
Root-Maggot Fly *Anthomyia pluvialis*
Noon Fly *Mesembrina meridiana*
Common Housefly *Musca domestica*
House Fly *Graphomya maculata*
Yellow Dungfly *Scathophaga stercoraria*
Bluebottle *Calliphora vomitoria*
Greenbottle *Lucilia caesar*
Cluster Fly *Pollenia rudis*
Fleshfly *Sarcophaga carnaria*
Tachinid Fly *Tachina fera*
Tachinid Fly *Eriothrix rufomaculata*
Common Green Colonel *Oplodontha viridula*
Soldier Fly *Beris clavipes*
Ornate Brigadier *Odontomyia ornata*
Broad Centurion *Chloromyia formosa*
Downlooker Snipefly *Rhagio scolopacea*
Common Horsefly *Haemotopata pluvialis*
St Mark's Fly *Bibio marci*
Spotted Mosquito *Culiseta annulata*
Common Mosquito *Culex pipiens*
Chironimid Midge *Chironomus plumosus*

Winter Gnat *Trichocera annulata*
Great Cranefly *Tipula maxima*
Common Cranefly *Tipula oleracea*
Spotted Cranefly *Nephrotoma appendiculata*
Cranefly *Ctenophora atrata*

ANTS, BEES AND WASPS
Black Garden Ant *Lasius niger*
Common Red Ant *Myrmica rubra*
Field Digger Wasp *Mellinus arvensis*
Sand Wasp *Ectemnius continuus*
European Beewolf *Philanthus triangulum*
European Hornet *Vespa crabro*
Common Wasp *Vespula vulgaris*
German Wasp *Vespula germanica*
Wall Mason Wasp *Ancistrocerus parietum*
Early Mining Bee *Andrena haemorrhoa*
Mining Bee *Andrena clarkella*
Mining Bee *Andrena praecox*
Nomad Bee *Nomada leucopthalma*
Hairy-footed Flower Bee *Anthrophora plumipes*
Cuckoo Bee *Melecta albifrons*
Honey Bee *Apis mellifera*
White-tailed Bumblebee *Bombus leucorum*
Buff-tailed Bumblebee *Bombus terrestris*
Common Carder Bee *Bombus pascuorum*
Early Bumblebee *Bombus pratorum*
Garden Bumblebee *Bombus hortorum*
Red-tailed Bumblebee *Bombus lapidarius*
Forest (Four-coloured) Cuckoo Bee *Bombus sylvestris*
Vestal Cuckoo Bee *Bombus vestalis*
Barbutt's Cuckoo Bee *Bombus barbutellus*
Hill Cuckoo Bee *Bombus rupestris*
Tree Bumblebee *Bombus hypnorum*
Ruby-tailed Wasp *Chrysis ignita*

Oak Apple Gall Wasp *Biorhiza pallida*
Robin's Pincushion Gall Wasp *Diplolepsis rosae*
Artichoke Gall Wasp *Andricus fecundator*
Knopper Gall Wasp *Andricus quercusradicis*
Spangle Gall Wasp *Neuroterus numismalis*
Spangle Gall Wasp *Neuroterus quercusbaccarum*
Chalcid Wasp *Pteromalus puparum*
Ichneumon Wasp *Lissonota setosa*
Ichneumon Wasp *Amblyteles armatorius*
Ichneumon Wasp *Ichneumon stramentarius*
Ichneumon Wasp *Pimpla hypochondriaca*
Yellow/Ophion Wasp *Ophion luteus/obscuratus*
Cimbicid Sawfly *Zaraea fasciata*
Turnip Sawfly *Athalia rosae*
Sawfly *Rhodogaster viridis*
Figwort Sawfly *Tenthredo scrophulariae*
Sawfly *Tenthredo livida*

FISH
Common Pike *Esox lucius*
European Eel *Anguilla anguilla*

REPTILES AND AMPHIBIANS
Smooth Newt *Triturus vulgaris*
Common Toad *Bufo bufo*
Common Frog *Rana temporaria*
Grass Snake *Natrix natrix*
Common Lizard *Lacerta vivipara*

BIRDS
Red-legged Partridge *Alectoris rufa*
Grey Partridge *Perdix perdix*
Common Pheasant *Phasianus colchicus*
Taiga Bean Goose *Anser fabalis*
Pink-footed Goose *Anser brachyrhynchus*

Greylag Goose *Anser anser*
Greater White-fronted Goose *Anser albifrons*
[Lesser White-fronted Goose *Anser erythropus*]
[Snow Goose *Chen caerulescens*]
Canada Goose *Branta canadensis*
[Barnacle Goose *Branta leucopsis*]
[Red-breasted Goose *Branta ruficollis*]
Mute Swan *Cygnus olor*
Whooper Swan *Cygnus cygnus*
Tundra (Bewick's) Swan *Cygnus bewickii*
Egyptian Goose *Alopochen aegyptiaca*
Common Shelduck *Tadorna tadorna*
Gadwall *Anas strepera*
Eurasian Wigeon *Anas penelope*
Mallard *Anas platyrhynchos*
Northern Shoveler *Anas clypeata*
Northern Pintail *Anas acuta*
Eurasian Teal *Anas crecca*
Common Pochard *Aythya ferina*
Tufted Duck *Aythya fuligula*
Common Goldeneye *Bucephala clangula*
Smew *Mergellus albellus*
Common Merganser (Goosander) *Mergus merganser*
Little Grebe *Tachybaptus ruficollis*
Red-necked Grebe *Podiceps grisegena*
Great Crested Grebe *Podiceps cristatus*
Eurasian Bittern *Botaurus stellaris*
Grey Heron *Ardea cinerea*
Little Egret *Egretta garzetta*
Northern Gannet *Morus bassanus*
Great Cormorant *Phalacrocorax carbo*
Western Osprey *Pandion haliaetus*
Eurasian Sparrowhawk *Accipiter nisus*
Western Marsh Harrier *Circus aeruginosus*
Hen Harrier *Circus cyaneus*

Montagu's Harrier *Circus pygargus*
Red Kite *Milvus milvus*
Common Buzzard *Buteo buteo*
Common Kestrel *Falco tinnunculus*
Merlin *Falco columbarius*
Hobby *Falco subbuteo*
Peregrine *Falco peregrinus*
Water Rail *Rallus aquaticus*
Common Moorhen *Gallinula chloropus*
Eurasian Coot *Fulica atra*
Common Crane *Grus grus*
Eurasian Oystercatcher *Haematopus ostralegus*
Pied Avocet *Recurvirostra avosetta*
Northern Lapwing *Vanellus vanellus*
European Golden Plover *Pluvialis apricaria*
Common Ringed Plover *Charadrius hiaticula*
Little Ringed Plover *Charadrius dubius*
Eurasian Woodcock *Scolopax rusticola*
Common Snipe *Gallinago gallinago*
Black-tailed Godwit *Limosa limosa*
Whimbrel *Numenius phaeopus*
Eurasian Curlew *Numenius arquata*
Spotted Redshank *Tringa erythropus*
Common Redshank *Tringa totanus*
Common Greenshank *Tringa nebularia*
Green Sandpiper *Tringa ochropus*
Wood Sandpiper *Tringa glareola*
Common Sandpiper *Actitis hypoleucos*
Dunlin *Calidris alpina*
Ruff *Philomachus pugnax*
Black-headed Gull *Larus ridibundus*
Mediterranean Gull *Larus melanocephalus*
Mew (Common) Gull *Larus canus*
Herring Gull *Larus argentatus*
Lesser Black-backed Gull *Larus fuscus*

Great Black-backed Gull *Larus marinus*
Little Gull *Larus minutus*
Common Tern *Sterna hirundo*
Common Pigeon *Columba livia*
Common Wood Pigeon *Columba palumbus*
Stock Dove *Columba oenas*
Collared Dove *Streptopelia decaocta*
Turtle Dove *Streptopelia turtur*
Common Cuckoo *Cuculus canorus*
Barn Owl *Tyto alba*
Tawny Owl *Strix aluco*
Short-eared Owl *Asio otis*
Little Owl *Athene noctua*
Common Swift *Apus apus*
Common Kingfisher *Alcedo atthis*
Lesser Spotted Woodpecker *Dendrocopos minor*
Great Spotted Woodpecker *Dendrocopos major*
European Green Woodpecker *Picus viridis*
Eurasian Jay *Garrulus glandarius*
Eurasian Magpie *Pica pica*
Western Jackdaw *Corvus monedula*
Rook *Corvus frugilegus*
Carrion Crow *Corvus corone*
Bohemian Waxwing *Bombycilla garrulus*
Marsh Tit *Poecile palustris*
Coal Tit *Parus ater*
Great Tit *Parus major*
Blue Tit *Cyanistes caeruleus*
Bearded Reedling (Tit) *Panurus biarmicus*
Woodlark *Lullula arborea*
Eurasian Skylark *Alauda arvensis*
Barn Swallow *Hirundo rustica*
Common House Martin *Delichon urbica*
Sand Martin *Riparia riparia*
Cetti's Warbler *Cettia cetti*

Long-tailed Tit *Aegithalos caudatus*
Willow Warbler *Phylloscopus trochilus*
Common Chiffchaff *Phylloscopus collybita*
Sedge Warbler *Acrocephalus schoenobaenus*
Eurasian Reed Warbler *Acrocephalus scirpaceus*
Common Grasshopper Warbler *Locustella naevia*
Eurasian Blackcap *Sylvia atricapilla*
Garden Warbler *Sylvia borin*
Lesser Whitethroat *Sylvia curruca*
Common Whitethroat *Sylvia communis*
Common Firecrest *Regulus ignicapilla*
Goldcrest *Regulus regulus*
Eurasian Wren *Troglodytes troglodytes*
Eurasian Nuthatch *Sitta europaea*
Eurasian Treecreeper *Certhia familiaris*
Common Starling *Sturnus vulgaris*
Ring Ouzel *Turdus torquatus*
Common Blackbird *Turdus merula*
Fieldfare *Turdus pilaris*
Redwing *Turdus iliacus*
Song Thrush *Turdus philomelos*
Mistle Thrush *Turdus viscivorus*
European Robin *Erithacus rubecula*
Common Nightingale *Luscinia megarhynchos*
Black Redstart *Phoenicurus ochruros*
Whinchat *Saxicola rubetra*
European Stonechat *Saxicola torquata*
Northern Wheatear *Oenanthe oenanthe*
Spotted Flycatcher *Muscicapa striata*
House Sparrow *Passer domesticus*
Eurasian Tree Sparrow *Passer montanus*
Dunnock *Prunella modularis*
Yellow Wagtail *Motacilla flava*
Grey Wagtail *Motacilla cinerea*
White (Pied) Wagtail *Motacilla alba*

Meadow Pipit *Anthus pratensis*
Water Pipit *Anthus spinoletta*
Common Chaffinch *Fringilla coelebs*
Brambling *Fringilla montifringilla*
Eurasian Bullfinch *Pyrrhula pyrrhula*
European Greenfinch *Chloris chloris*
Common Linnet *Linaria cannabina*
Common Redpoll *Acanthis flammea*
Common Crossbill *Loxia curvirostra*
European Goldfinch *Carduelis carduelis*
Eurasian Siskin *Spinus spinus*
Yellowhammer *Emberiza citrinella*
Common Reed Bunting *Emberiza schoeniclus*
Snow Bunting *Plectrophenax nivalis*

MAMMALS
Western Hedgehog *Erinaceus europaeus*
Common Shrew *Sorex araneus*
Common Mole *Talpa europaea*
Common Pipistrelle *Pipistrellus pipistrellus*
Greater Noctule *Nyctalus noctula*
Brown Long-eared Bat *Plecotus auritus*
Red Fox *Vulpes vulpes*
Stoat *Mustela erminea*
Weasel *Mustela nivalis*
[American Mink *Mustela vison*]
European Otter *Lutra lutra*
Common Seal *Phoca vitulina*
Grey Seal *Haliochoerus grypus*
[Chinese Water Deer *Hydropotes inermis*]
[Reeves' Muntjac *Muntiacus reevesi*]
[Grey Squirrel *Sciurus carolinensis*]
Bank Vole *Clethrionomys glareolus*
Northern Water Vole *Arvicola terrestris*
Field Vole *Microtus agrestis*

Harvest Mouse *Micromys minutus*
Wood Mouse *Apodemus sylvaticus*
Brown Rat *Rattus norvegicus*
House Mouse *Mus musculus*
Brown Hare *Lepus europaeus*
Rabbit *Oryctolagus cuniculus*

Index